PRACTICE TEST

FOR THE
SOCIAL WORK LICENSING EXAM:
EXAM THREE

SOCIAL WORK TEST PREP

Practice test for the social work licensing exam: exam three / Social Work Test Prep
ISBN: 978-0-9973855-3-3 (pbk)

1. Test preparation 2. Social work

Contents

Welcome

Welcome to SWTPs ASWB Practice Test for the Social Work Licensing Exam: Exam #3. Thanks for studying with us. By purchasing this book, you've taken a big step toward a goal you've likely been pursuing since you entered the field: social work licensure.

In these pages, you'll find guidance about what to expect on the ASWB exam and how best to approach it. The heart of the book is 170 exam questions, answers, and rationales, designed to help you increase your ease with social work exam content and with the test-taking process. The exam in this book is identical to one that appears on socialworktestprep.com (ASWB Exam #3).

To get access to the online version of the exam, just send proof of purchase (e.g., your Amazon receipt) to info@socialworktestprep.com—we'll help make it happen.

On the SWTP website, you'll also find several more exams available for purchase. Click around for additional exam-prep support, including our free Study Guide for the Social Work Licensing Exam, *which includes some of what follows on the next few pages—exam basics, study tips, and additional resources.*

Exam Basics

The Association of Social Work Boards (ASWB) administers the social work licensing exam for the entire U.S. and Canada. Exams come at four levels: Bachelors, Masters, Advanced Generalist, and Clinical. The ASWB has posted detailed outlines for each on their site (aswb.org). The credentials earned by passing the ASWB exam can be different from state to state. Most common are LSW, LMSW, LGSW, and LCSW (see your state board for those specifics).

The exam is comprised of 170 multiple choice questions. You get four hours to take the test. Of the 170 exam items you'll face, 150 count toward your score. The other 20 are testers—questions being tried out for use in a future exam. Our advice: since there's no way to know which exam items are testers, pretend you don't know this and approach each question as if it counts. If you hit an exam item that seems especially impossible, take your best guess and brush it off, telling yourself, "That one probably didn't count. On to the next!"

Study Guidelines

You may be feeling overwhelmed by all the studying ahead. Yes, there's an enormous amount of information that *could* show up on the exam. But what *actually* shows up on the exam is likely to be narrower, simpler, and easier to prepare for.

The people putting together social work licensing exams want to make sure that licensed social workers are compassionate, ethical, law-abiding professionals. They commission questions designed to test for those qualities. That means exam questions will tend to present real-world, close-call, social work situations. You may be able to answer many of them without preparing at all. Just go with your social work gut.

Some basic guidelines when attacking each new exam question: Remember that doing no harm and operating within scope of practice is essential. Knowing the *NASW Code of Ethics* well can help you through the majority of questions on the exam.

- Asking yourself, "What would the by-the-book perfect social worker do in this situation?" can often help shake loose a correct answer. Your real-life experience will help you pass the exam. But your knowledge that not all textbook answers apply in the real world is best left at the examination-room door. For the exam, think like an unjaded, optimistic, can-do social worker.
- Exam questions are generally straightforward and trick-free. If an answer seems obvious to you, that's probably because you know your stuff. Select that answer and move on to the next. If it seems impossibly convoluted, maybe it's a tester and won't count toward your score. Don't sweat it.
- The exam is meant to test for *beginning* social work skills. If an answer seems especially exotic and unfamiliar—something you haven't encountered in school or at work—look for something simpler.
- Try not to get rattled by questions asking for the BEST intervention or the MOST likely diagnosis. Even if it seems like it's yelling at you, it's still just a basic question about social work practice.

How do you apply all this? The best way to prepare is to practice. Practice gets you familiar with the rhythms of the test and gives you a chance to begin burning off test anxiety. You've purchased an SWTP Practice Test; you're off to a great start!

Keep in mind, you've made it this far. This exam won't be the hardest thing you've ever faced or ever will face. You can get it done!

Four Tips for Studying

1. **Take Care of Yourself**. It's easy to get worked up about the licensing exam. It's big, it's expensive, it doesn't always seem relevant to social work practice. Keep tabs on the effect that preparing for the exam is having on you. It's a whole additional stressor added onto your probably already sufficiently stress-filled day-to-day. Self-care will help. Maybe dial up the anxiety-reducing basics—sleep, breathe, eat, exercise. You know best what works for you.

2. **Focus on fundamentals.** The social work exam is meant for beginning professionals. That limits the amount of material worth studying. Study smart by mastering the material you are fairly certain you'll encounter on the exam. Learn the *NASW Code of Ethics*—it's the underpinning of the vast majority of exam questions. Know the common diagnoses in the *DSM*, the essentials of human development theory—that sort of stuff. Review scope of practice, mandated reporting, and suicide assessment. The examiners are looking to make sure you'll do a reasonably professional job and keep clients safe. If you've got that down, you're very close to passing the exam.

3. **Don't overstudy**. If you find yourself deep in the theoretical or diagnostic weeds as you're preparing for the exam, get out! Remember tip #2. And #1 while you're at it. All a lot of the questions require is social work-informed common sense. Take care not to cram and clutter your mind with unnecessary detail.

4. **Practice.** How do you know you've done all of the above? Take real-time, full-length practice exams like the one in this volume to help you gauge your readiness, identify areas you need to strengthen, and generally get acquainted with the experience of a four-hour, 170-question sit. At four hours, the licensing exam is more like a marathon than a sprint. Practice tests are like practice runs for athletes. They really help.

Exam Prep Resources

Get our free Study Guide to the Social Work Licensing Exam *when you create an account at socialworktestprep.com. In the guide, you'll find live links to resources listed below, help with managing anxiety, additional practice questions, and lots more. These are invaluable resources as you're preparing for the exam.*

Essential Review

If there's something you need to know for the exam that can't be found on the web, we have yet to discover it. Here are some essentials:

- *The NASW Code of Ethics* (free on the NASW website, socialworkers.org). There's nothing more important to have a good grasp on. Will this be on the test? Yes!
- *ASWB.org* contains basics about what to expect on the test—browse the site for exam outlines and pass rates.
- *NASW Standards of Practice* (free at socialworkers.org). Freshen up on the basics of social work practice.
- The *DSM-5* is, of course, going to come in handy as you continue studying. For exam prep purposes, we prefer the shorter desk reference edition. Also find *DSM-5* details on Wikipedia and elsewhere on the web.

Your MSW program textbooks are also a great resource. Board question writers are required to cite published sources for each item they submit. What are they likely to use? Their MSW program textbooks.

Additional Review

Have the essentials down? The suggested study links that accompany each question in online versions of SWTP practice exams are a great next step toward deeper review. For additional exposure to exam-related content, try browsing these sites:

- *Social Work Today Magazine* (socialworktoday.com). The "Eye on Ethics" column is a great primer on the very issues that often appear in exam questions.
- *The Social Work Podcast* (socialworkpodcast.com). Early episodes about different theories are especially helpful.
- *The New Social Worker* (socialwork.com). Includes articles covering a wide range of social work topics.

And of course, take a look at SWTP's long-running blog for additional free practice, test-taking research, success stories, and more.

Thanks again for preparing with SWTP. Happy studying and good luck on the exam!

Practice Questions

1. A social worker meets with a 65-year-old woman who reports that she has recently been unable to enter her second bedroom because it is full with her collection of old newspapers and magazines. What diagnosis should the social worker consider FIRST?

A) Hoarding disorder

B) Excoriation disorder

C) Major depressive disorder

D) Obsessive-compulsive disorder

2. The diagnoses autistic disorder, Asperger's disorder, childhood disintegrative disorder, and pervasive developmental disorder NOS are combined into which of the following in DSM-5?

A) Neurodevelopmental disorder

B) Autism spectrum disorder

C) Pervasive development disorder

D) Autistic disorder

3. A social worker meets with a 16-year-old boy and his parents. The teenager has recently been expelled from school because of multiple offenses, such as smoking on school property and fighting. The teenager was failing his classes and has an assault charge pending. His parents report feeling their son is depressed. The teenager states he has no problems and no need for meeting with the social worker. What is MOST evident here?

A) The teenager lacks insight.

B) The teenager has grandiose thoughts.

C) The teenager has below-average intelligence.

D) The teenager is a concrete thinker.

4. A client says to the social worker, "None of my friends like me anymore. I tried to call three of them last night. I left messages but no one called me back. I think they probably all got together and decided they should stop being friends with me." The thoughts the client is having are an example of:

A) Obsessive thinking

B) Catastrophic thinking

C) Delusional thinking

D) Magical thinking

5. It's appropriate to use a provisional diagnosis when:

A) A client doesn't quite meet the criteria for a particular diagnosis.

B) When the social worker is determining whether a client's symptoms stem from substance abuse as opposed to a psychiatric disorder.

C) The client's symptoms have not been present for at least three months.

D) The client doesn't have health insurance, so there's no need for a regular diagnosis.

6. A social worker receives a referral for a person diagnosed with paranoid personality disorder. What is the social worker likely to encounter when working with this person?

A) Detachment and hostility, since the client is likely to assume the social worker has hidden motives.

B) An overly dramatic and emotional presentation combined with a need for constant reassurance.

C) Difficulty regulating emotions, thoughts, and impulsive behaviors.

D) An inability to recognize social cues and an emotionally cold and indifferent attitude.

7. Dissociative disorders usually stem from:

A) Personality disorders

B) Physical health issues

C) Anxiety disorders

D) Childhood trauma

8. A social worker meets with a 75-year-old client who is concerned about her recent increase in problems with forgetfulness and confusion. She's says she's not depressed, but can't seem to focus on things as well as she once could. What diagnosis should the social worker first consider?

A) Dementia

B) Probable vascular neurocognitive disorder

C) Mild neurocognitive decline

D) Alzheimer's disease

9. A social worker provides consultation to a local preschool program. She notices that a four-year-old boy tends to flinch when approached by adults, and cries when his parents come to pick him up as well. On an occasion when the preschool teacher praises the boy's school behavior, the mother comments that the boy tends to save all his "evil" behavior for home. What is MOST likely indicated here?

A) The child may be a victim of sexual abuse.

B) The child may be a victim of physical abuse.

C) The child likely has some developmental delays.

D) The child may be a victim of neglect.

10. A social worker meets with a woman diagnosed with bipolar disorder I. The woman reports that she's been staying in bed much of the time recently, because she feels too depressed to face the day. While she's in bed, she uses her laptop to look for bus tickets to random places where she might move, but her racing thoughts make it difficult for her to follow through with purchasing the tickets. What is MOST likely happening with this woman?

A) She's experiencing a depressive episode.

B) She's experiencing a hypomanic episode.

C) She's experiencing a mixed episode.

D) She's experiencing a manic episode.

11. A mother takes her ten-year-old son to see a social worker because the child has not attended school in the past three weeks. The mother states that her son went to school without incident for the first two months, but lately pleads to be allowed to stay home. What is the MOST likely reason for the child's school refusal?

A) Depression

B) Anxiety

C) Attention deficit hyperactivity disorder

D) Oppositional defiant disorder

12. Delusions of grandeur are most commonly associated with:

A) Mood disorders.

B) Schizophrenia.

C) Histrionic personality disorder.

D) Borderline personality disorder.

13. Adolescents with bipolar I disorder:

A) May be at increased risk for exploitation due to disinhibited behavior.

B) Are likely misdiagnosed because it is rare in young people.

C) Do not experience manic episodes.

D) Are likely to excel in academics because of their increased energy levels.

14. Studies have shown that people with irritable bowel syndrome are likely to suffer from:

A) Illness anxiety disorder

B) Somatic symptom disorder

C) A personality disorder

D) Generalized anxiety disorder

15. Which of the following is considered an impulse control disorder?

A) Kleptomania

B) Bipolar disorder

C) Erotomania

D) Obsessive-compulsive disorder

16. A client attends an intake appointment at the social worker's office. The client initially sits down but soon begins walking around the room while answering questions. The client also exhibits handwringing. What is the BEST way for the social worker to describe the observations in the mental status exam?

A) Poor concentration

B) Anxious behavior

C) Psychomotor retardation

D) Psychomotor agitation

17. What is the main difference between cyclothymic disorder and bipolar disorder?

A) People with cyclothymia have more severe mood swings than people with bipolar disorder.

B) People with cyclothymia only experience depressive episodes and do not experience hypomanic episodes.

C) People with cyclothymia only experience manic episodes and not depression.

D) Mood swings are less severe in cyclothymia than in bipolar disorder.

18. A man gets scolded by his boss for being late for work. For the rest of the day, he behaves in an especially friendly manner toward his boss, and works through his lunch break. What defense mechanism is this man MOST likely using?

A) Sublimation

B) Compartmentalization

C) Reaction formation

D) Undoing

19. A social worker meets with a woman whose relationships tend to last no more than three weeks. Initially, she tells the social worker, she'll describe her new partner as the "best person I've ever met," but within a few weeks tends to say things such as, "He's selfish and doesn't care about how I feel." This type of behavior is MOST common with which diagnosis?

A) Obsessive compulsive personality disorder

B) Antisocial personality disorder

C) Borderline personality disorder

D) Dependent personality disorder

20. Common symptoms of paranoid personality disorder include:

A) Rapidly shifting shallow expression of emotions.

B) Persistent belief that a lover is cheating.

C) Auditory and visual hallucinations.

D) Hoarding objects with little or no monetary value.

21. A school social worker receives a referral from the physical education teacher. A ten-year-old girl has started refusing to change her clothes in the locker room with the other girls. This behavior may be a symptom of:

A) Conduct disorder

B) Sexual abuse

C) Neglect

D) ADHD

22. Which of the following comorbidities is the most common with ADHD?

A) Bipolar disorder

B) Sleeping disorders

C) Eating disorders

D) Learning disorders

23. A college student meets with a social worker because he has a problem with numbers. He states that he needs things to end on an even number; if class ends at 45 minutes past the hour, he won't get up from seat until the clock shows 46 minutes. He states that odd numbers are "bad" and he fears something bad will happen if he ignores them. What is the MOST likely diagnosis?

A) Schizophrenia

B) Obsessive-compulsive disorder

C) Specific phobia

D) Delusional disorder

24. Which of the following treatments is an example of aversion therapy to treat alcohol addiction?

A) Alcoholics Anonymous

B) Antabuse

C) Methadone

D) Electroconvulsive therapy

25. The main difference between schizophrenia and schizophreniform disorder is:

A) Schizophreniform disorder includes abnormal moods in addition to psychosis, while schizophrenia doesn't involve abnormal moods.

B) Schizophreniform disorder includes a lack of interest in social relationships while people with schizophrenia enjoy social relationships.

C) In schizophreniform disorder, the symptoms have lasted less than six months; in schizophrenia, the symptoms have lasted six months or more.

D) Schizophrenia is more typical in adults while schizophreniform disorder occurs during adolescence.

26. A social worker in an outpatient mental health clinic meets with a new client. What is the BEST way to determine a client's level of judgment?

   A) Ask the client to explain the meaning of a proverb such as, "A rolling stone gathers no moss."

   B) Ask the client a question, such as "What would you do if you found a pair of car keys sitting on the ground in the parking lot of a grocery store?"

   C) Ask the client directly whether or not he thinks he has good judgment.

   D) Ask the client to memorize four objects and recall those objects after five minutes.

27. A client tells a social worker, "I feel so frustrated that my husband doesn't help around the house. He says he works too hard at his job to come home and do any cleaning." Which of the following responses is the BEST example of active listening?

   A) "Should we discuss how your resentment is likely to lead to other problems in your relationship?"

   B) "You feel angry that you have to bear all of the responsibility at home."

   C) "Your husband believes men should be the breadwinners and shouldn't have to do household chores."

   D) "You feel frustrated that your husband doesn't feel he should have to help out around the house."

28. During an intake assessment, a social worker asks a client to memorize four unrelated objects, then moves on to other questions. Five minutes later, the social worker asks the client to recall those four objects. What information is the social worker MOST LIKELY trying to obtain?

   A) The social worker wants to assess the client's intelligence.

   B) The social worker wants to examine the client's short-term memory.

   C) The social worker wants to examine the client's remote memory.

   D) The social worker is attempting to examine the client's ability to manage stress.

29. A social worker at a community mental health center is meeting with a client for the first time. The social worker wants to test the client's abstract thinking. What question would BEST evaluate the client's ability to think abstractly?

A) How are dogs and cats alike?

B) Can you name the last four presidents of the United States?

C) Have you ever felt your mind was playing tricks on you?

D) Who is the president of the United States?

30. A mother takes her four-year-old daughter to meet with a social worker. The mother says the family experienced a house fire, and though everyone got out safely, she thinks her daughter may be traumatized as a result. The family is now staying with the mother's parents until they can rebuild. What would be the BEST question to determine if the child might have PTSD?

A) Ask the child if she likes living with her grandparents.

B) Ask the child if she worries about fires.

C) Ask the mother if the child is adjusting to the new living situation.

D) Ask the mother if the child engages in repeated play reenacting the fire.

31. A social worker is conducting an initial assessment on a woman who has decided to seek help for her grief. As the woman describes her brother's murder, she smiles and laughs throughout the account. What should the social worker note in the mental status exam?

A) Euthymic affect

B) Flat affect

C) Blunted affect

D) Inappropriate affect

32. A social worker in a community mental health center meets with an eight-year-old child and his grandmother to conduct a biopsychosocial assessment. The child was recently placed with his grandmother by child protective services because of his mother's substance-abuse problem. During the initial interview, the grandmother focuses on the mother's long-term heavy drinking, and states she doesn't think the mother will ever be able to get the child back. When the social worker asks about the child's background and history, the grandmother continues to focus on the mother's drinking. What is the BEST way for the social worker to proceed?

A) The social worker should ask the grandmother to leave the session and interview the child alone.

B) The social worker should stop asking questions and let the grandmother use the session to discuss her concerns.

C) The social worker should focus the interview on what the grandmother wants to discuss by asking more questions about the mother's drinking.

D) The social worker should underscore the purpose for gathering background information and continue asking questions.

33. A busy primary care practice employs ten doctors and two social workers. The doctors have noticed that many of their patients with somatic complaints actually have underlying depression, but don't always have time to assess a person's mental health and then refer them for social work services during the appointment. What is the BEST way for the office to identify depressed patients who may benefit from social work services?

A) Posters should be placed in the lobby encouraging patients to ask for a social work referral if they're depressed.

B) All patients could be given a depression screening to help identify those who may be suffering from depression.

C) The reception staff should begin asking patients if they'd like to speak with a social worker.

D) The office should hire more social workers, so that each patient can be interviewed about possible symptoms of depression.

34. The difference between a screening and an assessment is:

A) A screening requires specialized training and expertise and an assessment is used to determine a diagnosis.

B) An assessment usually consists of yes or no questions and a screening defines the extent of the problem.

C) A screening determines the diagnosis and the assessment establishes recommendations to address the problem.

D) A screening evaluates the possible presence of a problem and an assessment defines the nature of a problem.

35. A social worker conducting an initial assessment asks the client if she's ever driven to perform behaviors as a result of repeated, unwanted thoughts. What is the social worker MOST likely to trying to learn?

A) The social worker wants to know if the woman is autistic.

B) The social worker wants to know if the woman has a specific phobia.

C) The social worker wants to know if the woman has flashbacks, such as those found in PTSD.

D) The social worker wants to know if the woman has any compulsions, such as those found in OCD.

36. A social worker receives a referral from child protective services for a 35-year-old woman. Child protective services removed the woman's children from her care because they had evidence that the woman's boyfriend was sexually abusing the children. When the social worker meets with the woman for the initial assessment, how should the social worker use the information received from child protective services?

A) The social worker should neither read the reports nor acknowledge receiving them.

B) The social worker should give the reports to the woman to read so she can say what is true and what isn't.

C) The social worker should tell the woman the reports have been received and ask her to tell the story from her point of view.

D) The social worker should read the reports but not let the woman know the information was received.

37. A college student meets with a social worker on campus. The student states she has difficulty paying attention during class, is easily distracted when doing homework, has trouble staying organized, and loses items frequently. What question would MOST help the social worker determine if the student might have ADHD?

A) Are you hyperactive?

B) How often do you drink alcohol?

C) How long have you been experiencing these problems?

D) Do you have difficulty sleeping?

38. A school social worker meets with a 14-year-old boy. The boy states that several nights ago he and some other boys spray-painted graffiti on the side of a building. Upon learning this information, what obligation does the social worker have?

A) The social worker is obligated to report the crime to the police department.

B) The social worker is obligated to notify the teen's parents.

C) The social worker is obligated to keep the information confidential.

D) The social worker is obligated to notify the school of the incident.

39. A 15-year-old boy tells a social worker he thinks most of his problems started when his stepfather came into his life. He states he sometimes fantasizes about murdering his stepfather, but denies having a plan to kill him. How should the social worker respond?

A) The social worker should make a report to child protective services.

B) The social worker should maintain the client's confidentiality.

C) The social worker has a duty to warn the stepfather.

D) The social worker should tell the boy's mother.

40. A social worker has been meeting with a woman who is experiencing stress as a single parent. During a regularly scheduled appointment, the woman acknowledges slapping her daughter across the face and hitting her son with a belt. She states she is very sorry and is certain she will not do this again. How should the social worker handle this?

A) Inform the woman of the obligation to report the incident to child protective services and continue to work with her on ways to reduce her stress.

B) Since the woman has acknowledged the abuse, the abuse is now a treatment issue, and there's no need to report it to child protective services.

C) Make a call to child protective services without telling the woman, since disclosure may damage the therapeutic relationship and discourage the woman from seeking further help.

D) Contact the children's guidance counselor at school and request the children be interviewed to see what their side of the story is.

41. A social worker is seeing a client who has just been charged with murder. The social worker is contacted by a reporter who wants to know whether or not the client has a mental illness. The reporter states that he contacted the client in jail and the client confirmed that he sees the social worker for treatment. How should the social worker respond?

A) The social worker should decline to confirm whether or not the person is a client.

B) The social worker should tell the reporter that the client will need to sign a release of information prior to any discussion.

C) The social worker can confirm that the client has been in treatment but should not offer any details.

D) Since it's a public safety issue, the social worker has the discretion to disclose information about the client's treatment.

42. According to HIPAA, communicating with clients via email and sending information to other agencies via fax is:

A) Only allowable for non-identifiable information.

B) Allowable with certain safeguards in place.

C) Never allowed.

D) Always allowed.

43. A social worker has been in private practice for ten years. The social worker shares office space with two other social workers and two receptionists. What is the BEST way for the social worker to store the files of clients who have been discharged?

A) The social worker should keep the records where the office staff and other social workers in the building can have access if necessary.

B) The social worker should keep the files locked up in a place where no one else will have access.

C) Social workers should ship old records to a third-party storage agency.

D) Since inactive files should be purged one year after discharge, the social worker shouldn't be storing old records.

44. A school social worker receives a referral for an eight-year-old girl who is very disruptive in class. After a couple of months of weekly meetings, the girl discloses that her uncle, who often visits the home, has been sexually abusing her for about a year. Who should be made aware of this disclosure?

A) Child protective services only

B) Child protective services and the child's parents

C) Child protective services, the teacher who referred the child, and the child's parents

D) Child protective services and the school department

45. A social worker is providing outpatient substance-abuse services to a woman who has been diagnosed with alcohol abuse. The woman reports that one night last week while she was drinking, her six-year-old daughter tried to dump her alcohol down the drain. The client states that she slammed her daughter's head into the floor repeatedly out of anger. The woman states she would have never done anything like this sober, she's stopped drinking, and swears she'll never drink again. How should the social worker respond?

A) The social worker must make a mandatory report to child protective services.

B) The social worker should refrain from making a report, because the woman is being treated for substance abuse, which allows this woman a higher level of confidentiality.

C) The social worker should document the incident, and if it happens again, make a report to child protective services.

D) Since the woman states she's stopped drinking, the social worker doesn't need to make a report to child protective services.

46. A social worker conducts couples therapy with a husband and wife. After several sessions, the couple separate. The social worker receives a request from the man's attorney for the social worker's treatment records. The man has signed a release of information for any and all records. What should the social worker do FIRST?

A) The social worker should call the wife and ask if she wants the records released.

B) The social worker should release records to both the husband and wife and not give them to a third party.

C) The social worker should provide all the records when asked to do so.

D) The social worker should seek legal consultation about how to proceed.

47. A social worker receives an invitation to a surprise birthday party for a friend. The party will be held at one of the social worker's client's homes. How should the social worker respond to the invitation?

A) The social worker should talk with the client about the awkward situation and ask that the party be moved somewhere else.

B) The social worker should attend the party because not attending may hurt the client's feelings.

C) The social worker should decline the invitation by saying there is a conflict of interest, without stating the precise nature of the conflict.

D) The social worker should decline the invitation without revealing that the host is a client.

48. A social worker has been working with a woman for several months. The woman has an upcoming court date to address custody issues regarding her child. The social worker receives a call from the woman's lawyer, who wants the social worker's opinion about this woman's ability to successfully parent her child. The social worker should FIRST:

A) Tell the lawyer that nothing will be discussed until a subpoena is received.

B) Provide written copies of the woman's treatment goals.

C) Obtain a release of information from the woman before talking to the lawyer.

D) Discuss only facts with the lawyer, and not offer any opinions.

49. A social worker meets with a woman for an initial assessment. The woman reports symptoms of depression that began recently, and states she was married twice. When the social worker asks about those marriages, the woman says she doesn't want to talk about them. How should the social worker proceed?

A) In order to encourage the client to talk about her marriages, the social worker should explain the importance of discussing past relationships.

B) Since the woman's past relationships aren't likely to be related to her current depression, the social worker should respect her right to privacy and not ask any further questions.

C) The social worker should end the interview and tell the woman she can resume when she feels ready to talk.

D) The social worker should tell the woman that without a thorough assessment, it's unlikely her depression can be treated successfully.

50. A social worker met with a woman who shared some recent suicidal ideation. The client refused to go to the emergency room, and the social worker allowed her to return home. The social worker is uncertain whether she did the right thing, and chooses to consult a colleague about the incident. In terms of revealing the client's name, what should the social worker do?

A) The social worker should reveal the client's name so they can both document that the social worker sought consultation.

B) The social worker can reveal the client's name only if the colleague works for the same agency.

C) The social worker should not reveal the client's name or any identifying information about the client.

D) It is acceptable to reveal the client's name to a colleague since it involves a safety issue.

51. When a social worker provides clinical supervision to another social worker, what is the supervisor's liability?

A) A supervisor who doesn't have direct contact with the client doesn't have any liability.

B) A clinical supervisor can be held liable for inadequate or negligent supervision.

C) A clinical supervisor only has liability if the supervisor is also the agency supervisor.

D) Supervisors can only be sued by the supervisee and cannot be held liable by the client.

52. A social worker conducts an assessment on a man with a substance-abuse problem. The social worker doesn't have expertise in substance abuse and feels the client will be best served by being transferred to someone else. The social worker is aware of two social workers in the area who do substance-abuse treatment, one of whom the social worker has worked closely with and whose expertise the social worker especially trusts. How should the social worker proceed when giving information about referral options?

A) The social worker should recommend the client find someone with substance-abuse expertise, but not offer any names.

B) The social worker should offer only the name of the person the social worker especially trusts.

C) The social worker should offer both names, but discuss why the social worker prefers one over the other.

D) The social worker should offer the client the names of the two social workers, and remain neutral about both.

53. A social worker has been meeting with a self-referred man who has a history of depression and alcoholism. Besides addressing his substance abuse and mental health with the social worker, the man attends AA meetings, and sees a counselor mandated by his probation. In terms of collaboration, what is the MOST important thing the social worker should do?

A) The social worker should consult with the client's probation officer to see what sort of counseling the man is receiving.

B) The social worker should consult with the client's insurance company to ensure that services aren't being duplicated.

C) The social worker should consult with the other counselor to ensure that services are not being duplicated.

D) The social worker does not need to collaborate with other professionals, since the client's other counseling is part of a court order.

54. A social worker receives a referral for a client whose employee assistance program only allows for three therapy sessions. In addition to lacking health insurance and other financial issues, the client has a lengthy history of trauma, is currently going through a divorce, and is having problems at work. The social worker tends to use art therapy and narrative therapy as principal treatment modalities. What is the BEST way for the social worker to proceed?

A) The social worker should treat the client the same way that anyone with health insurance would be treated.

B) The social worker should warn the client prior to her first session that she will most likely need long-term therapy and may have to pay out of pocket.

C) The social worker should refer the woman to someone who has expertise in solution-focused or other short-term therapies.

D) The social worker should try to do her usual treatment in three sessions.

55. A 25-year-old man meets with a social worker because he is embarrassed by his premature ejaculation. He is in a fairly new but serious relationship and thinks it is impacting their love life. What is the FIRST thing the social worker should do?

A) Instruct him on the "squeeze technique" to help him learn to delay orgasm.

B) Refer him to a sex therapist, especially if the social worker lacks expertise in this area.

C) Recommend he meet with his primary care physician to rule out any biological causes.

D) Recommend his partner attend treatment with him, since this issue is best dealt with as a couple.

56. A clinical social worker has been in practice for seven years. The social worker works full-time at a community mental health center. As part of best practice, how much supervision should the social worker receive?

A) The social worker should receive supervision on an "as needed" basis.

B) The social worker should receive one hour of supervision for every 18 hours of direct service work.

C) After seven years of clinical practice, the social worker does not need any supervision.

D) The social worker should receive one hour per week of supervision.

57. A social worker consults with a supervisor after a particularly difficult session with a client. The supervisor suggests the social worker begin doing process recordings with the client. Which of the following is the supervisor specifically recommending?

A) Use a two-way mirror so other social workers can observe the sessions.

B) After each session write down word for word everything the social worker can recall.

C) Bring a tape recorder to each session with the client and record what is said.

D) Videotape each session, with the client's permission.

58. When a social worker meets with a clinical supervisor, what are the recommendations regarding documentation?

A) There's no need to document clinical supervision.

B) Both the supervisor and the supervisee should document clinical supervision.

C) The supervisor should carefully document the topics covered in supervision.

D) The social worker receiving supervision can choose to take notes as desired.

59. A social worker receives a phone call from a client who's been meeting with the social worker for several months. The client is crying and tells the social worker that she was raped by a neighbor earlier in the day. What should the social worker do FIRST?

A) The social worker should recommend the client come to the office for an immediate appointment.

B) The social worker should recommend the client contact the police.

C) The social worker should make a mandated report to the police to report the crime.

D) The social worker should recommend the client seek immediate medical attention.

60. Which of the following is an example of an administrative supervisor's duty?

A) Discussing how the agency's policies impact the supervisee's service to clients.

B) Making suggestions about a social worker's treatment interventions.

C) Discussing the supervisee's approach to treatment planning.

D) The supervisor helps reduce job stress so the social worker can provide services more effectively.

61. An outpatient social worker meets with a man who has been diagnosed with schizophrenia. The man takes medication and states he finds it helpful. He continues to report strong beliefs in paranormal activity and attends weekly meetings with others who share his beliefs. How should the social worker proceed with this man's treatment?

A) The social worker should include discussions about the man's belief systems and how it may or may not relate to his symptoms.

B) The social worker should treat the schizophrenia without addressing the man's reports of paranormal activity.

C) The social worker should consider the client's beliefs in paranormal activity as symptoms of his schizophrenia.

D) The social worker should discourage the man from attending groups who believe in paranormal activity, since such beliefs can fuel his symptoms.

62. A child in a Latino family is being picked on by peers. The child's teacher has reported the child exhibits some behavior problems. In a typical, traditional Latino family, the person MOST likely to address the problems with the school is:

A) The grandmother.

B) Both parents together.

C) The father.

D) The mother.

63. Taijin kyofusho and shenjing shuairuo are examples of:

A) Japanese mental illnesses

B) Holistic medications

C) Culture-specific syndromes

D) Depressive syndromes

64. A social worker meets with a Russian immigrant who was referred by his primary care physician. The social worker asks the man whether or not there's a family history of mental illness. The man refuses to answer. How should the social worker proceed?

A) The social worker should stress the importance of obtaining information about the family's history of mental illness.

B) Ask the man why he won't answer the question.

C) Make note of the man's choice not to answer and move on to the next question.

D) The social worker should ask the question in another way to make sure the client understands what information is being sought.

65. Which of the following is true of culture-bound syndromes?

A) Culture-bound syndromes have been incorporated throughout DSM-5.

B) Attention to specific cultural presentation has been dropped in DSM-5.

C) Culture-bound syndromes are no longer diagnosed because they're a function of people's culture and not their mental health.

D) Culture-bound syndromes can only be diagnosed by a physician, since they refer to physical health issues.

66. A mother refers her six-year-old son to a social worker. During the initial intake, the mother, who is biracial, says her son is racist. She states that he regularly says things like "White people are better." She wants the social worker to address this issue with her son. How should the social worker respond?

A) Explain that racial stereotyping is part of normal identity development in children with biracial parents.

B) Agree to educate the child about race and equality.

C) Inquire about where the child may be learning these attitudes.

D) Explain that the child is likely making racist comments to get attention.

67. Accepting gifts from clients:

A) May be acceptable depending on the client's culture.

B) Is never acceptable.

C) Is always acceptable.

D) Is only acceptable if the client insists.

68. A social worker meets with a five-year-old child and his parents. The parents are concerned about the child's oppositional behavior. Asking about the parents' cultural beliefs during the intake:

A) Would be inappropriate in front of the child, so the social worker should first ask the child to leave the room.

B) Would only be appropriate if the social worker suspects their beliefs about parenting fall outside the social norm.

C) Would be appropriate, because the parents' culture can influence their parenting practices.

D) Would be inappropriate, because the family may assume the social worker is blaming the child's behavior on cultural issues.

69. A social worker meets with a family who moved to the United States from Mexico 10 years ago. The social worker asks questions such as, "In what language are the TV programs you watch?" and "Throughout your adult life, have most of your neighbors been Mexican Americans?" What is the MOST likely reason that the social worker is asking these questions?

A) The social worker is determining how much of a language barrier is likely present.

B) The social worker is trying to determine if the family is in the United States legally.

C) The social worker is trying to establish rapport with the family.

D) The social worker is trying to learn about the family's degree of acculturation.

70. A social worker meets with parents and a teenager who was born male but identifies as female. The teen wants to begin transitioning socially to a female by wearing female clothing and requesting being called "she." The parents want the teen to identify as male, because they'are greatly concerned about bullying and safety. How should the social worker proceed?

A) Since the parents disagree with the teenager, the social worker should discourage the social transition, which will most likely increase family conflict.

B) The social worker should discourage the teen from making the social transition until adulthood.

C) The social worker should help the teenager and the parents weigh the pros and cons of making the social transition.

D) The social worker should begin helping the teen with the social transition.

71. A hospital social worker meets with a family--a mother, father, 12-year-old boy and 8-year-old girl. The 12-year-old boy has been diagnosed with muscular dystrophy and his health has declined to the point that he requires the use of a wheelchair much of the time. The mother used to work as a nurse but became a stay-at-home parent when their son became ill. The father has recently stopped working due to a back injury. What is one of the MOST important issues the social worker should check in to see how the child's illness is affecting this family?

A) The social worker should determine if the parents are experiencing caregiver fatigue and see if they have enough support to help them care for their son.

B) The social worker should see if the 8-year-old daughter is experiencing any behavioral issues due to her brother's illness.

C) The social worker should see if the child's school is meeting his educational needs and whether the family needs help advocating for their son.

D) The social worker should see if the 12-year-old child is experiencing any side effects from his medications.

72. Which of the following is true about methylphenidate (Ritalin)?

A) Ritalin is a sedative that is commonly prescribed for ADHD.

B) Ritalin was banned from the marketplace as a result of black box warnings.

C) Ritalin is a stimulant commonly prescribed for ADHD.

D) Ritalin is not safe for children under the age of 18.

73. People who complete suicide usually:

A) Have some type of mental illness or substance-abuse problem.

B) Do not have any sign of prior mental illness.

C) Have borderline personality disorder.

D) Under the age of 18.

74. A social worker meets with a nine-year-old child and her parents. The parents report the child is anxious, complains of a stomach ache in the mornings and tries to miss the bus to school. They say the anxiety has increased so for the past two weeks they have allowed her to stay home from school. What should the social worker recommend FIRST?

A) The social worker should recommend the parents find a tutor to help the child stay caught up on her school work.

B) The social worker should recommend the child return to school as soon as possible.

C) The social worker should advocate for the child with the school to see how the child's needs can be met.

D) The social worker should recommend that the child continue to stay home until she has made enough progress in treatment to return to school.

75. A 50-year-old man with cirrhosis of the liver was referred to a social worker by his primary care physician. The man drinks up to four cans of beer per day. He states he doesn't think alcohol is a problem, and denies his liver is as bad as his doctor says. The social worker assigns the man homework to help him cut down on his alcohol consumption, but the man never completes his homework and continues to drink at the same rate. What is MOST likely happening?

A) The social worker hasn't helped the man gain enough social support to help him quit drinking.

B) The man likely doesn't understand his homework assignments and his refusal to participate is the result of his confusion.

C) The man is most likely precontemplative and isn't ready to commit to making any changes.

D) The man is most likely contemplative about his drinking but not yet ready to commit to change.

76. Treating combat veterans for PTSD can be complicated, owing to difficulties encountered during exposure therapy. A successful treatment modality for many soldiers has included:

A) Psychoanalytic therapy.

B) Virtual reality therapy.

C) Sand tray therapy.

D) Hypnotherapy.

77. Six students at the same rural high school have died by suicide over the past two years. This high rate of suicide is MOST likely to:

A) Be a risk factor that can lead to increased suicides by other people in the community.

B) Not influence the suicide rate in the community one way or the other.

C) Only affect the suicide rate if the previous suicides were interrelated.

D) Be a protective factor leading to decreased suicide in the community.

78. Being raised by a single mother places children MOST at risk for:

A) Low IQ and academic problems.

B) ADHD and bipolar disorder.

C) Developmental delays and peer problems.

D) Poverty and physical health problems.

79. Which of the following underlying theories are a basis for cognitive-behavioral therapy?

A) Family systems theory.

B) Psychodynamic theory.

C) Conflict theory.

D) Social learning theory.

80. Which of the following is considered a protective factor for suicide?

A) Being unmarried.

B) Being male.

C) Being over the age of 70.

D) Having children in the home.

81. Which of these is true about the short-term effects of marijuana?

A) Increased energy and confidence, involuntary teeth-clenching, and blurred vision.

B) Tremors, vertigo, muscle twitches, paranoia, and anxiety.

C) Relaxed muscles, increased heart rate, and a distorted sense of time.

D) Increased respiration, increased physical activity, and irregular heartbeat.

82. A social worker begins meeting with a woman who states her husband has abused her verbally for the past 15 years, and physically for the last two. This is the first time she has reached out for help. According to a family systems perspective, what is MOST likely to happen initially if this woman tries to become more assertive?

A) The husband will become more aggressive in an attempt to maintain homeostasis.

B) A second order change is likely to take place.

C) The husband won't change his behavior.

D) The husband will become less aggressive in an attempt to give his wife more freedom.

83. A mother meets with a social worker because her ten-year-old son has been exhibiting unusual, sexualized behavior. The mother is concerned that he may have been sexually abused. What might the social worker tell the mother regarding the most common characteristics of perpetrators?

A) Perpetrators are often females in a position of authority, such as teaching.

B) The majority of perpetrators are family members who are under the age of 18.

C) Most perpetrators are adult males who are known and trusted by the child.

D) Most perpetrators are males who meet their victims over the Internet.

84. A social worker meets with a recently widowed man. The man says his dog seems very sad and lonely since the wife's death. What defense mechanism is the man MOST likely exhibiting?

A) Repression

B) Projection

C) Denial

D) Compartmentalization

85. A mother meets with a social worker because she is worried about her 16-year-old son's substance abuse. She reports catching him smoking marijuana several times. He says pot is "not a big deal" and is not interested in seeking help. What is the BEST suggestion the social worker can make to ensure the mother does not enable her son?

A) The social worker should advise the mother to stop spending time with her son as punishment for his drug use.

B) The social worker should advise the mother to stop giving her son an allowance, since he might use the money to buy drugs.

C) The social worker should advise the mother to take her son to see a substance abuse counselor whether he wants to or not.

D) The social worker should advise the mother to kick her son out of the house immediately until he has quit using drugs.

86. Personality disorders are MOST likely caused by:

   A) Childhood trauma.

   B) A combination of factors, including genetics, childhood trauma, and peer relationships.

   C) Genetics.

   D) Peer relationships.

87. Reactive attachment disorder is primarily caused by:

   A) Genetics.

   B) A child's behavior problem that causes caregiver stress.

   C) Neglect, a parent's emotional unavailability or disruption in caregivers.

   D) Sexual abuse or physical abuse.

88. A social worker conducts an assessment on a seven-year-old boy. The boy's parents state that he doesn't listen, he's having trouble in school, and his out-of-control behavior is causing marital distress for his parents and academic problems for his 12-year-old sister. From a family systems perspective, what is MOST likely happening?

   A) The family hierarchy is such that the boy has equal power with his parents.

   B) The boy's mental illness is causing the parents' marital distress.

   C) The boy is the scapegoat for the family's problems.

   D) The older sister likely has more problems than her parents realize.

89. A social worker has been meeting with an elderly man in a nursing home. The man states he just learned his teenage grandson was severely beaten by another teenager. The man says he would like to hunt down the other teenager and shoot him. How should the social worker respond FIRST?

   A) The social worker should validate the man's feelings of anger and question whether or not he has any further intent.

   B) The social worker should contact the police so the victim can be notified that a threat was made against his life.

C) The social worker should notify the nursing home staff of the man's threats so they can keep him under high alert.

D) The social worker should remind the man that making such threats can lead to serious consequences.

90. A school social worker meets with a 13-year-old girl. The girl states that she keeps getting into trouble because her peers "dare" her to do things or because she follows the crowd. She regrets many of her decisions and states she wants to "get things back in order." What intervention is likely to be the MOST helpful?

A) Teaching her assertiveness skills.

B) Reviewing her earliest experiences of being peer-pressured.

C) Exploring her feelings of guilt.

D) Conducting a group intervention with her friends.

91. A social worker focusing on what the client wants his future life to be like is using which therapeutic approach?

A) Solution focused

B) Existential

C) Object Relations

D) Psychoanalytic

92. One of the most effective interventions for people with antisocial personality disorder is:

A) Cognitive behavioral therapy, focusing on irrational thinking.

B) The use of peer communities to confront behavior and promote change.

C) Family therapy with an emphasis on addressing past attachment issues.

D) A humanistic approach that offers unconditional positive regard.

93. An oncology social worker is working with a family in which the teenage daughter has been diagnosed with a rare but terminal form of cancer. The girl and her parents are hopeful for a miracle, despite hearing from the oncologist that the cancer is terminal. Given the family's reaction, how should the social worker proceed?

A) The social worker should meet separately with the teenager to ensure she understands the cancer is terminal.

B) The social worker should gently remind the girl and her family that the cancer is terminal.

C) The social worker should help the family focus on their optimism.

D) The social worker should help the family move through the other stages of grief, since they're most likely in denial.

94. Habit reversal is a technique that has shown to be effective in treating:

A) Trichotillomania

B) Attention deficit hyperactivity disorder

C) Obsessive-compulsive disorder

D) Specific phobias

95. A social worker meets with a 70-year-old man who meets the criteria for major depression. The man lives alone and has been experiencing increased physical health problems. During the initial interview, the MOST important thing is for the social worker to:

A) Gather personal and family history.

B) Determine if the client needs help doing activities around his home.

C) Assess the client's risk for suicide.

D) Determine the client's strengths.

96. A social worker meets with the family of a 23-year-old man who has been hospitalized for bizarre behaviors at work, and subsequently diagnosed with schizophrenia. What type of intervention is likely going to be MOST helpful for the family at this time?

A) The social worker should conduct family therapy that includes the client, so the family can process what led to his admission.

B) The social worker should educate the family about the man's diagnosis and what they might expect in the future.

C) The social worker should discuss group home options with the family, since the man will likely need ongoing support.

D) The social worker should give the family information about obtaining guardianship of the man.

97. The purpose of a psychoeducational substance-abuse group is MOST likely to:

A) Help members identify and discuss how their early life experiences contribute to their substance abuse.

B) Help precontemplative or contemplative people develop a need to seek help by educating them about their disorder and the recovery options.

C) Help members identify and change maladaptive thoughts and behaviors in order to maintain sobriety.

D) Help people maintain sobriety and gain self-esteem by discussing their daily struggles with other members of the group.

98. A man seeks help from a social worker after the death of his wife from a brief illness. The man states he feels intense sadness and asks how long he should expect the grief to last. How should the social worker respond?

A) Tell him that it takes about one year to recover from the loss of a spouse.

B) Tell him that intense grief usually lasts about six months.

C) Explain that grief is different for everyone and there's no predictable time frame.

D) Explain that most widowers remarry in about three years.

99. A social worker meets with a man who has a long history of severe alcohol abuse. The man states he has significantly cut back on his drinking over the past few years, but still drinks one or two beers daily. He's been with his girlfriend for over a year, and she's started attending AA with him. He states he's pleased about her show of support. Involving his girlfriend in treatment with the social worker:

A) Would likely threaten the social worker's therapeutic alliance with the client.

B) Is likely to increase the client's commitment to change and could be helpful to his treatment.

C) Would likely only be helpful if his girlfriend has successfully recovered from her own substance-abuse issues in the past.

D) Would be inappropriate, because the client may feel the social worker and his girlfriend are ganging up on him.

100. A social worker meets with a blended family that consists of a mother and biological teenage son, her husband and his biological teenage son, and a six-year-old child the couple had together. The social worker asks a family to create a "family sculpture." The purpose of family sculpting is MOST likely to:

A) Establish goals and create behavioral changes.

B) Help the family resolve conflict without talking about it.

C) Look for solutions to the issues surrounding a blended family.

D) Identify each person's role in the family and their relational patterns.

101. Asking a client to recount traumatic memories over and over again:

A) Is likely to retraumatize a client and should never be done.

B) Desensitizes a client when done in conjunction with relaxation training.

C) Should never be in done in outpatient settings because it can lead to increased suicide risk.

D) Should only be done under hypnosis.

102. A social worker at a long-term care facility is MOST likely to perform which of the following duties?

A) Inviting a local girl scout troop to sing to the residents and arranging for a podiatrist to visit patients at the facility.

B) Documenting residents' medication and researching ways for the establishment to save money.

C) Interviewing nurses applying for direct care positions and educating them about patients' needs.

D) Establishing policies to reduce safety risks for residents unable to ambulate, and developing emergency preparedness plans.

103. A couple has been meeting with a social worker for three weeks. They report wanting to work on their marriage. Despite the social worker's attempts to set rules, they argue constantly over small details. The social worker responds by saying, "You two are really good at arguing." The social workers response is an example of:

A) Functional family therapy.

B) Unethical behavior.

C) Solution focused therapy.

D) A paradoxical intervention.

104. A social worker meets with a blended family comprised of a mother and her 10-year-old son from a previous marriage, her second husband, and his 14-year-old son. Whenever the social worker asks the man a question, the woman tries to speak for her husband. The social worker changes seats and sits between the woman and the man. What intervention is the social worker likely using?

A) Joining, a part of family therapy

B) Exposure therapy, a part of behavioral therapy

C) Boundary marking, a part of structural family therapy

D) Shaping, part of behavior modification

105. A man tells a social worker that he cheated on his wife. He states it only happened once, and his wife is not aware of the incident. He asks the social worker for his professional opinion about whether or not he should tell his wife about the infidelity. How should the social worker respond?

A) The social worker should advise the man based on the social worker's own values.

B) The social worker should recommend that the man begin couples therapy with his wife to address underlying marital issues.

C) The social worker should help the man weigh the pros and cons of telling or not telling his wife.

D) The social worker should advise the man to tell his wife, since keeping secrets will be harmful to his marriage.

106. A social worker meets with a 25-year-old woman who has recently been diagnosed with bipolar I. The woman describes having manic episodes that cause her to drive recklessly and engage in promiscuous sex. She states she has also had depressive episodes during which she was unable to get out of bed, and lost her job as a result. She's been placed on a mood stabilizer and says her mood now seems to be consistent. What intervention is likely to be MOST helpful to this client?

A) Psychoanalytic therapy to help her address past issues that are likely contributing to her mood.

B) Assertiveness training and advocacy to help her get her job back now that she's stabilized.

C) Teaching self-monitoring skills so she can recognize warning signs of mood changes and triggers.

D) The empty-chair technique in gestalt therapy, where she can learn to talk to her body about her symptoms.

107. A social worker meets with a 25-year-old man who has Asperger's syndrome. He's fairly successful at his job as a biologist, but spends much of his time socially isolated, and feels depressed. The man says he's tried online dating, but after one or two dates, women usually tell him they just want to be friends. What sort of treatment is this man MOST likely to benefit from?

A) Supportive counseling that gives him a chance to talk about his feelings.

B) Exposure therapy to reduce his anxiety about social situations.

C) Social skills training to help reduce his isolation.

D) Medication to reduce his depression.

108. A woman tells a social worker she doesn't bother to apply for jobs anymore because she won't get hired anyway. The social worker tells her to practice telling herself, "If I complete at least two job applications every day, it will increase the likelihood I'll find work." What technique is the social worker MOST likely using?

A) Cognitive restructuring

B) Mindfulness

C) Behavior therapy

D) Advocacy

109. A clinical social worker in an outpatient behavioral health center meets with a 30-year-old woman who reports a lot of anxiety and stress. She receives a monthly disability check but has difficulty managing her finances, which she says are the main source of her stress. The social worker detects the woman has some cognitive limitations and may be taken advantage of financially by others. What should the social worker do FIRST?

A) Recommend the woman take budgeting and finance classes through the local community center.

B) Establish a monthly budget with the woman and assist her in following it.

C) Explain to the woman that she needs a payee who can manage her money for her.

D) Refer this woman for a neuropsychological evaluation to see if she's able to manage her finances on her own.

110. A woman meets with a social worker because her four-year-old son has some behavioral issues, including constant whining. The social worker asks the woman how she responds to her son's whining. The woman says she tells him to stop but he doesn't listen. If the social worker is a firm believer in behavior modification, what is the MOST likely suggestion the social worker would make?

A) The social worker would recommend the mother redirect the child's attention.

B) The social worker would recommend the mother validate the child's feelings.

C) The social worker would recommend the mother ignore the child's whining.

D) The social worker would recommend the mother help the child identify his feelings.

111. A social worker has been meeting with a depressed woman for several months. The social worker encourages the woman to keep a journal. Each session they talk about her feelings, in order to help the woman gain a better understanding of herself. What intervention is the social worker MOST likely using?

A) Psychoanalysis

B) A humanistic approach

C) Cognitive behavioral therapy

D) Solution-focused therapy

112. Which of the following usually begin during childhood or adolescence and are categorized as a neurodevelopmental disorder in DSM-5?

A) Anxiety disorders

B) Mood disorders

C) Psychotic disorders

D) Tic disorders

113. A social worker meets with a mother who has recently learned that her daughter was sexually abused by her stepfather, the woman's second husband, over a period of at least two years. The woman states she feels angry that her daughter disclosed the abuse to a guidance counselor instead of telling her. What information can the social worker tell the mother that might be helpful to her understanding why her daughter didn't tell?

A) Children usually feel more comfortable disclosing abuse to a professional rather than a parent.

B) Children sometimes don't disclose abuse to a parent, because of fears they won't be believed or the family might be destroyed.

C) Children almost always tell someone outside the family first before telling a parent.

D) Children usually tell someone at school, since they believe the information will be kept confidential.

114. A doctor has referred a woman to a social worker because the woman has been diagnosed with vaginismus. The treatment goals are MOST likely to address:

A) The woman's anxiety about having sex.

B) The woman's hypersexuality.

C) The woman's sexual promiscuity.

D) The woman's lack of sexual desire.

115. A social worker meets with several clients at a local nursing home. A new resident to the facility has Parkinson's disease. What symptoms is the person likely to exhibit?

A) Significant vision problems, loss of bowel control, depression, and memory problems.

B) Tremors, impaired balance, monotone speech, and hesitation prior to speaking.

C) Disorientation, wandering, delusions, and loss of inhibitions.

D) Difficulty recognizing faces, decreased vision, and increased difficulty to adapt to low light levels.

116. Common symptoms during the beginning stages of Alzheimer's include:

A) Incontinence and difficulties with mobility.

B) Loss of previous skills such as reading and writing.

C) Short-term memory loss and difficulty solving problems.

D) Long-term memory loss and delusions.

117. A social worker serves as a consultant to a local preschool program. The staff express concern about a four-year-old foster child who is very friendly with strangers. The child will often hug the parents of other children or start conversations with visitors to the preschool. What is MOST likely the reason for the child's behavior?

A) The child most likely has an intellectual disability.

B) The child may have disinhibited social engagement disorder.

C) The child is likely an extrovert, so the behavior does not warrant concern.

D) The child may have reactive attachment disorder.

118. A hospital social worker is looking for a nursing home placement for an elderly woman. The woman has had a serious stroke and is no longer able to communicate or care for herself. What is the FIRST thing the social worker should do to help determine an appropriate placement for the woman?

A) See if the patient has a spouse who is available to sign paperwork.

B) Determine if the patient has a health care proxy or living will in place.

C) Meet with any available family members to obtain necessary signatures.

D) Speak with doctors about obtaining emergency guardianship for the patient.

119. A 60-year-old man meets with a social worker in a community mental health center. The man states that he was widowed five years ago. He has started dating and was hoping to become intimate with his new partner. However, he has been experiencing erectile dysfunction for the first time, and wonders if it may be related to the guilt he feels about dating again. What should the social worker do FIRST?

A) Recommend couples counseling with the man's partner to address their sexual issues.

B) Recommend a physical exam with his primary care doctor to rule out physical health issues.

C) Explain that this is part of the normal aging process.

D) Establish treatment goals to resolve the man's underlying grief.

120. A 14-year-old has been diagnosed with conduct disorder. The teenager also has a substance abuse problem. What disorder is the child MOST at risk for developing as an adult?

A) Major depression

B) Histrionic personality disorder

C) Antisocial personality disorder

D) Narcissistic personality disorder

121. A hospital social worker meets with family members of an 85-year-old woman with Alzheimer's disease. The woman's daughter would like to have her mother move in with her, because her mother is no longer able to care for herself. The daughter asks what things she can do to help care for her mother in her home. What is the MOST appropriate suggestion?

A) The social worker should discuss ways in which the woman can teach her mother to perform tasks safely, such as using a microwave instead of the stove.

B) The social worker should discuss ways of keeping the woman's mother from being bored or lonely, such as leaving the TV on a news channel during the day.

C) The social worker should discuss strategies--such as removing clutter--that the woman can use to make her home safer for her mother.

D) Because caring for a person with dementia is a big responsibility, the social worker should discourage the woman from having her mother move in.

122. Family therapy is usually LEAST appropriate in which of the following situations?

A) A 25-year-old woman requests her parents attend family therapy so they can better understand her depression.

B) A 30-year-old woman is struggling with alcohol problems and she and her husband are requesting family therapy.

C) Parents request family therapy because their 16-year-old daughter seems to be pulling away from them.

D) Parents request family therapy to help their newly adopted ten-year-old adjust to their home.

123. According to Erikson's psychosocial stages, if a child does not receive predictable and consistent care from a caregiver during his first year of life, he could be at risk for:

A) Isolation.

B) Guilt.

C) Inferiority.

D) Mistrust.

124. A social worker meets with an adult male with mild intellectual disability. The man resides with his parents but states his goal is to live independently. He tells the social worker that he has met someone over the Internet and his plan is to move in with this person, even though they have never met. How should the social worker proceed?

   A) The social worker should help the client identify what services he will need when he moves.

   B) The social worker should point out potential risks associated with moving in with a stranger.

   C) The social worker should respect the man's right to self-determination and praise him for finding a way to live independently.

   D) The social worker should be outwardly supportive but should contact the man's family to discuss his plan.

125. A social worker is asked to serve on a board of directors at a local homeless shelter. The social worker would need to attend meetings outside normal business hours. The social worker is interested in the opportunity, which would be strictly voluntary. What is the BEST way for the social worker to respond to the request?

   A) The social worker can participate, because social workers are encouraged to offer some services without pay.

   B) The social worker should agree to serve on the board, but only if the board will provide salary and malpractice coverage.

   C) The social worker should not engage in volunteer work as a professional, because it could expose the social worker to malpractice.

   D) The social worker should decline the request, because working more hours without pay will likely lead to burnout.

126. A social worker is employed in a medical facility. The social worker's role is to meet with people prior to their medical appointment and conduct any necessary screenings. When meeting with pregnant women, the social worker only asks about any current drug use when the patient is of a lower socioeconomic status. The social worker's actions:

A) Are a good way to avoid offending middle- or upper-class women.

B) Show how a provider's values can interfere with appropriate screenings.

C) Are an efficient way to gather information, because women of higher socioeconomic status aren't likely to use drugs.

D) Are based on evidence-based practices.

127. A social worker volunteers at a local charity. One of the other volunteers invites her out on a date. The social worker knows this man is a brother of one of her current clients. What are the ethical implications for engaging in a romantic relationship with this man?

A) The social worker should decline to go on the date, since it's likely to compromise the therapeutic relationship with the client.

B) The social worker should ask her client how he would feel if she went out on a date with his brother.

C) The social worker is free to accept the invitation, but should talk to her client about how to ensure it doesn't impact their therapeutic relationship.

D) Since the man is not her client, the social worker is free to engage in a romantic relationship with him.

128. While testifying in court, a social worker is asked her opinion about whether or not the defendant, her client, is capable of physically abusing her child. The social worker is MOST likely:

A) Acting outside of her scope of practice.

B) A witness for the prosecution.

C) Breaching confidentiality.

D) An expert witness.

129. An eight-year-old child has started seeing a social worker. The social worker and the client's mother have agreed on once-a-week sessions, but the mother has canceled so many appointments the social worker has only seen the child about once a month for four months. The social worker reiterates that more sessions are needed to help the child, but despite her promises, the mother hasn't yet brought the child consistently. How should the social worker proceed?

A) To increase the child's attendance, the social worker should tell the mother the child needs to meet two times per week rather than one.

B) The social worker should continue to see the child as often as the mother is able to take him to appointments.

C) Since the child isn't likely to benefit from being seen only once a month, the social worker should terminate the treatment.

D) The social worker should tell the family to take a month off and think about whether or not they want treatment.

130. A social worker is doing discharge planning at a medical hospital, referring patients to receive in-home care or nursing-home care following their discharge. A nursing home contacts the social worker, says they have several available beds, and offers the social worker a bonus for referring people to the nursing home. How should the social worker respond?

A) The social worker should decline any type of referral bonus from the nursing home.

B) The social worker should accept the nursing home's invitation to receive referral bonuses and make referrals accordingly.

C) The social worker can accept the referral bonus, but should not allow it to influence decisions as to where people are referred upon discharge.

D) The social worker should inform a supervisor that the social worker is receiving compensation for the referral.

131. Which of the following is considered unethical behavior?

A) Discharging clients who miss too many appointments.

B) Working only one day per week and not offering clients scheduling flexibility.

C) Charging clients for missed appointments.

D) Advising a client which medications he should ask his doctor to prescribe.

132. A couple considering divorce meets with a social worker. They report arguing constantly and feeling hopeless about preserving the marriage. What is important for the social worker to share with the couple with regard to informed consent?

A) The social worker should recommend they both seek legal counsel, since session notes could be used in court if they decide to divorce.

B) The social worker should recommend individual counseling in addition to couples counseling.

C) The social worker should inform the couple that counseling runs the risk of increasing their marital discord, especially at first.

D) The social worker should inform the couple that because their relationship has deteriorated, counseling is not likely to be helpful.

133. What should social workers be aware of in terms of malpractice cases?

A) Social workers cannot be sued for malpractice, but the company they work for can be.

B) Social workers can be sued for malpractice and should carry malpractice insurance.

C) Social workers can only be sued if they breach confidentiality.

D) The social work licensing board will defend social workers who face legal issues, so social workers don't need separate malpractice insurance.

134. A social worker employed by a hospital faces an ethical dilemma regarding confidentiality. The hospital's policy conflicts with the NASW Code of Ethics. How should the social worker resolve the ethical dilemma?

A) The social worker should try to resolve the issue in a manner consistent with the Code of Ethics and seek consultation if necessary.

B) The social worker should follow the hospital's policy in this instance but advocate for policy change in the future.

C) The social worker should resign from the hospital.

D) The social worker should comply with the hospital's policy even if it contradicts the Code of Ethics.

135. A hospice care social worker notices he's feeling overwhelmed by his work lately. He feels confused, exhausted, and has been having difficulty sleeping. The social worker suspects he may be experiencing burnout. What should he do FIRST?

A) The social worker should explain his burnout to his clients and apologize, since it's likely they haven't been getting good services lately.

B) The social worker should try to leave work an hour earlier so he doesn't feel so overwhelmed.

C) The social worker should consult with a supervisor to discuss a plan of action to address his burnout.

D) Since burnout often goes away within a few weeks, the social worker should wait to see if it passes in his case.

136. A dual relationship, in which a social worker interacts with a client on a social basis:

A) Always requires a transfer to a new social worker.

B) Is always unethical.

C) Might not be unethical if it isn't sexual in nature.

D) Should always be avoided.

137. A social worker has met with a man for six sessions to address his grief. The man's wife passed away two years ago and he still cries whenever he tries to talk about her. After the sixth session, the man calls the social worker to say he's not making progress and would like to transfer to a female social worker. What should the social worker do?

A) Agree to discharge him from treatment and tell him he's welcome to find a new social worker.

B) Tell the man that he should continue for at least 12 sessions before deciding if he's making any progress.

C) Explain that changing to a female social worker could be problematic since he's dealing with issues related to the loss of his wife.

D) Give the man several choices of female social workers and offer to refer him to the one he selects.

138. A residential treatment program treats people with a combination of mental health and substance- abuse problems. The severity of the clients' issues has created a lot of problems, including assaults on staff members. The program director has decided to offer a token economy system, in which residents can earn tokens for positive behaviors, such as medication compliance and participation in group therapy, exchanging the tokens for toiletries, movies, or phone cards. In terms of ethics, what should the facility keep in mind?

A) It's unethical to use a token economy system with adults, because the staff would be treating the residents like children.

B) It's unethical to link medication compliance to rewards, but appropriate to reward participation and compliance with other services.

C) It's unethical to make rewards contingent on the client's participation or compliance with the program.

D) So long as staff are well-trained and the program is voluntary, a token economy system is ethical.

139. A social worker meets with a 45-year-old woman who discloses she was physically abused by her father when she was a child. She states that her father used to beat her with a belt and sometimes threatened to kill her. In terms of mandated reporting to child protective services, what is the social worker's responsibility?

A) The social worker needs to make a mandated report based on this woman's reports of childhood abuse.

B) The social worker doesn't need to make a mandated report, because there's no evidence any children are in imminent danger.

C) The social worker should consult with a supervisor to discuss the pros and cons of making the mandated report.

D) The social worker doesn't have a legal obligation to make a report, but making a report would be the ethical response.

140. A social worker has started to engage in a romantic relationship with another person who works at the office. Which of the following is true of co-worker relationships?

A) Social workers can engage in a romantic relationship with co-workers, as long as potential conflicts of interest are avoided.

B) Social workers can engage in romantic relationships with any colleague, except for a supervisor.

C) Social workers are not allowed to engage in any romantic relationships with co-workers.

D) Social workers cannot engage in relationships with clients but are free to engage in relationships with any colleagues they wish.

141. Which one of the following is MOST likely a breach of ethical conduct?

A) Despite having a release of information for a psychiatrist, the social worker reviews the information with the client prior to releasing it.

B) The social worker has to cancel two appointments in a row due to illness.

C) A social worker discloses personal tragedy to a client.

D) A social worker discusses movies with a client.

142. A certain substance-abuse treatment program provides services to homeless people. Because their homelessness often interferes with their ability to attend outpatient services regularly, the social work director decides to offer housing to the people who attend the program, stipulating that anyone who tests positive for drugs will be immediately evicted. What are the ethical ramifications of making abstinence a stipulation for housing?

A) Making abstinence a condition for housing is ethical, but funding for such a program is likely to be impossible.

B) It's unethical to evict anyone for testing positive for drugs.

C) It's unethical to randomly drug test the people living in the housing units.

D) It's ethical to make abstinence a stipulation for housing.

143. A social worker is filling out a form for a client, in ink, that documents the client's diagnosis and treatment goals. The social worker incorrectly writes the diagnosis as generalized anxiety disorder, then remembers the diagnosis is actually social anxiety disorder. What is the BEST way for the social worker to deal with the error?

A) The social worker should put a line through the error, initial and date it, write the word "error," and then add the change.

B) The social worker should write a letter explaining the error and staple it to the original form.

C) Since the error can't be fixed, the social worker should ask the client for a new copy of the form.

D) The social worker should use white-out to cover up the mistake and then write the correct diagnosis.

144. A social worker works in a busy private practice. When a client fails to show for an appointment, in terms of billing, the social worker MOST likely:

A) Can only bill the insurance company if it's Medicaid.

B) Can only bill the insurance company for a partial amount.

C) Cannot bill the insurance company.

D) Can bill the insurance company for the full cost of the session.

145. A father takes his seven-year-old son to see a social worker in a community mental health center. The father states that his son is struggling to deal with the ongoing custody dispute. Currently the father has primary residence and the child visits with his mother every other weekend, but the mother wants primary residence and is taking the case back to court. The father thinks the child's mother may want the social worker to testify in court. What information should the social worker discuss with the child's father at the time of the assessment?

A) The social worker should volunteer to testify on the father's behalf.

B) The father should be made aware of the social worker's role in treatment and the potential conflict of interest if the social worker is subpoenaed.

C) The social worker should gather information about the child's best interest so a recommendation can be made to the court.

D) The social worker should offer to treat the child while evaluating what's in the child's best interest.

146. A client meets with a social worker to discuss a variety of issues. The client talks about past trauma, a substance abuse problem, relationship issues, and financial problems. The client goes back and forth between problems and seems overwhelmed, however, she continuously talks about how her relationship problem with her spouse is most troubling to her. Which intervention is likely to be MOST helpful in identifying treatment goals?

A) Creating a genogram

B) Supportive counseling

C) Reflective listening

D) Partializing

147. A social worker at an outpatient mental health center conducts an intake on an eight-year-old child. The family's life is too chaotic for the child to benefit from outpatient services. The social worker's current agency does not provide in-home services, so a referral to a different agency is indicated. What is the BEST way for the social worker to proceed?

A) If the family agrees to the referral, the social worker should make the referral, discharge the client, and follow up with the family to ensure the referral was successful.

B) Since the agency doesn't provide in-home services, the social worker should continue to provide outpatient services and try to meet the family's needs.

C) If the family agrees, the social worker should make the referral to the other agency and discharge the child from outpatient services.

D) The social worker should provide the family with the phone number for the agency that can provide in-home services, and encourage them to call.

148. A social worker in a rural practice setting has met with a client three times. During the fourth meeting, the client begins talking about her stepdaughter, whom the social worker now realizes he is also treating. Neither the woman nor her stepdaughter seems aware that they're both seeing the same therapist. How should the social worker proceed?

A) The social worker should transfer the woman to a new social worker and furnish her with names of available providers.

B) The social worker should explain the situation to the stepdaughter's biological mother and recommend the stepdaughter seek services elsewhere.

C) Since treatment has already begun, the social worker should continue to meet with the woman.

D) The social worker should hold a meeting with the woman and her stepdaughter to discuss treatment options.

149. A client is being treated for social phobia. When completing the treatment plan, the social worker wants to include objective data. Which one of the following treatment goals is based on objective data?

A) The client will attend church once a week.

B) The client will keep a journal that documents anxiety ratings on a daily basis.

C) The client will self-report reduced feelings of anxiety during therapy appointments.

D) The client will report a better understanding of anxiety.

150. A woman was referred to a social worker by her primary care physician because she has diabetes and doesn't take care to manage her blood sugar. The woman states she's depressed, forgets to test her blood sugar, and doesn't really like taking her medication. Who should establish the treatment goals for the treatment plan?

A) The physician who made the referral

B) The client

C) The social worker

D) The social worker and client

151. Providing clients with information on how to get help when you're away from the office, and giving them access to 24-hour daily coverage:

A) Is not usually practical because most social workers aren't able to offer such information.

B) Can reduce a client's risk for suicide and is part of best practice.

C) Can be unethical, because clients may become dependent on the 24-hour coverage rather than working through problems on their own.

D) Requires social workers to offer clients their personal phone numbers so they can be contacted in the event of an emergency.

152. A social worker meets with a client who is seeking treatment for generalized anxiety. The client is interested in including some non-traditional approaches to addressing the anxiety. What is the treatment plan MOST LIKELY to include?

A) Medication

B) Eye movement desensitization and reprocessing

C) Yoga and breathing techniques

D) Psychoanalytic therapy

153. A social worker is working with a client who has been diagnosed with PTSD after getting into a serious car accident. In the course of establishing treatment plan goals, the social worker stresses the importance of discussing the car accident in detail during therapy sessions. What is the social worker's MOST likely intent?

A) The social worker wants to help the client develop a story about the accident by using narrative therapy.

B) The social worker wants to use exposure therapy to reduce the client's distress about the accident.

C) The social worker is likely hoping to witness what coping skills the client uses when discussing distressing events.

D) The social worker wants to gather as much information as possible about the accident to gain a clear picture of the event.

154. A depressed client states he's not interested in taking medication to reduce his depression. The social worker recommends the client begin exercising as part of his treatment plan. The social worker's treatment recommendation is:

A) Inappropriate, since only the client's doctor should be recommending changes to the client's physical activity.

B) Likely to improve the client's overall physical health but unlikely to have any impact on the client's mental health.

C) Appropriate, since it's likely to help reduce the client's depression.

D) Risky, as the client may experience side effects that can actually increase the depression.

155. A social worker in a community mental health center has a caseload of about 30 active clients. The social worker plans to go on maternity leave for at least six weeks. How should the social worker handle this absence?

A) Each client should be given options about waiting, discharge, or referral to a different social worker.

B) Clients should be told the date when the social worker will be returning so they can resume treatment after her absence.

C) The social worker should provide clients with a phone number where she can be reached during her absence from the office.

D) Clients should be discharged and referred to social workers who will be able to continue their treatment.

156. A social worker meets with a man with a 25-year history of very heavy drinking. The man continues to drink daily but states he wants to quit. What level of care is likely MOST appropriate as a first step?

A) Self-help groups

B) Partial hospitalization program

C) Acute medical hospitalization

D) Residential treatment program

157. A social worker is employed as a case manager for a community mental health center. The agency is very busy and has recently been receiving increased referrals for case management. As a result, the social worker's caseload has doubled. What is the BEST way for the social worker to respond?

A) The social worker should advocate for a smaller caseload to ensure that everyone is getting the services they need.

B) The social worker should prioritize the new referrals by scheduling their initial appointments, even if it means that established clients will have to miss appointments.

C) The social worker should space out the clients' sessions to ensure that everyone can be seen, even if appointments can only take place every other week.

D) The social worker should seek professional consultation about which clients should be prioritized, to ensure that the social worker's feelings about clients aren't interfering with scheduling.

158. A social worker employed as a case manager works at a homeless shelter, helping families find affordable housing, and linking families to various mental health, substance-abuse, employment and social service programs. In terms of record keeping, what is the case manager's responsibility?

A) The social worker only needs to keep records if the client's insurance is being billed.

B) The social worker needs to keep client records and all case management activities need to be documented.

C) The social worker should keep statistical records to help the homeless shelter obtain funding.

D) Social workers who are employed as case managers do not need to keep any records.

159. The director of social work at an acute care hospital wants to evaluate the effectiveness of the department's social workers. What would likely be the BEST way for the director to measure each social worker's performance?

A) The director could randomly survey former patients and ask if they were satisfied with the social work services they received during their hospital stay.

B) The director could use criteria such as how many days patients remain inpatient after being medically discharged, as well as the amount of time it takes for patients to receive social work services.

C) The director could ask each social worker to complete a self-evaluation form.

D) The director could ask social workers to evaluate each other's performance.

160. A group of hospital social workers decide to give clients evaluation forms and comment cards after they've been discharged to learn more about their experience with treatment. Clients are told they don't have to fill out the forms or sign them. The social workers' actions are:

A) A good way to collect data to help evaluate their effectiveness.

B) Unethical, because clients shouldn't be asked to give feedback.

C) Not likely to be helpful, since clients aren't likely to give honest feedback.

D) Not likely to be helpful, because clients often feel worse after treatment and may rate the social workers' performance negatively.

161. A social worker in private practice decides to establish a rule barring contact with clients outside of their appointments. All scheduling and rescheduling issues will be handled by the receptionist, and all other issues will need to wait until the next appointment. Establishing such a rule:

A) Is a healthy boundary to set with all clients.

B) Is a good way to prevent social work burnout.

C) Can damage the therapeutic relationship.

D) Is a good way to ensure clients don't become overly dependent.

162. One of the best ways to make the termination process MOST successful is:

A) To link clients to social supports and review the gains made in treatment.

B) To allow the client to make decisions about when to end treatment.

C) To gradually decrease contact over the course of several months so that the client won't feel abandoned.

D) To keep treatment brief so that the client won't become dependent or overly attached.

163. A social worker is working with a woman who was physically and emotionally abused during her childhood by both her mother and father. The woman makes frequent comments to the social worker along the lines of, "I'm sure you'll lie to me like everyone else in my life." In the interest of building trust, what is the BEST way for the social worker to respond to this type of statement?

A) The social worker should set limits with the client, making it clear that such statements are not allowed.

B) The social worker should confront the client directly about these comments.

C) The social worker should offer to transfer the client to a different social worker.

D) The social worker should remain consistent and nonjudgmental to help the client gradually work through trust issues.

164. A social worker meets with a couple who have been experiencing relationship issues connected with the wife's heavy drinking. The husband states he frequently tells his wife to stop and sometimes tries to hide her alcohol. How should the social worker proceed?

A) Recommend that the husband seek individual treatment to learn how to stop enabling his wife.

B) Tell them they can't begin couples therapy until the wife gains control over her substance abuse.

C) Begin seeing them as a couple to address the substance-abuse problems and relationship issues.

D) Tell the couple they can return for treatment after they both attend 12-step meetings for one month.

165. An eight-year-old child has been meeting with a social worker each week for six months to address his trauma. The child was inside a building when a tornado hit and later developed symptoms of PTSD. The child's symptoms have resolved and he's met his treatment goals. What is the BEST way for the social worker to proceed?

A) The social worker should schedule a "graduation" appointment and celebrate the child's progress prior to discharge.

B) The social worker should continue to see the child weekly, because termination at this stage is likely to cause the child to regress.

C) The social worker should leave rescheduling open-ended, by telling the parent to call when a problem arises.

D) The social worker should space the child's sessions out to once a month so the child will continue to have support available.

166. When it comes to establishing boundaries in a therapeutic relationship, the social worker should:

A) Take each client's social and cultural factors into account when determining how to maintain healthy boundaries.

B) Offer the client a list of acceptable and unacceptable behaviors so the client is clear about boundaries.

C) Create a fixed list of rules about boundaries to ensure that violations do not occur.

D) Ask for the agency's policies on boundaries and follow those rules when developing a therapeutic relationship.

167. A social worker talks to a supervisor about a child who's been placed in foster care. Before the child was removed from home, the social worker made several reports to child protective services about neglect. The social worker states he recently had a dream about the client. What is the therapist MOST likely experiencing?

A) A dual relationship with the client.

B) A subconscious way of working out therapeutic issues with the child.

C) A normal reaction to the child's change in caregiver.

D) Countertransference about the child.

168. A social worker is working with a woman who discloses her long history of sexual abuse by an uncle. The woman says she's never told anyone about the abuse, largely due to her guilt and shame at having sometimes sought out her uncle and taken pleasure in the abuse. What is the BEST way for the social worker to respond to show empathy?

A) "Child abuse is never the child's fault."

B) "I know how you feel."

C) "You feel ashamed because there were times you liked the abuse."

D) "You shouldn't feel ashamed. You were just a child."

169. A social worker has been making progress with a woman who wants help managing her anxiety and depression. After several sessions, the woman reports that she got into a physical altercation with her boyfriend a few days ago. Her 7-year-old and 9-year-old children were present, and one was cut by flying debris of a plate broken during the fight. The social worker wants to make a report to child protective services. What can the social worker do to reduce the risk that making the report will damage the therapeutic relationship?

A) The social worker should inform the client that her children are in danger of being removed from her but remind the client that the social worker is there to help.

B) The social worker can give the woman a warning and tell her that if another incident happens, a report will need to be made.

C) The social worker can encourage the mother to make a self-report from the social worker's office.

D) The social worker should make the report anonymously so that no one will know the social worker made the report.

170. A social worker in an outpatient mental health center is using cognitive behavioral therapy to help a man with a history of depression and alcohol abuse. The man arrives for an appointment and appears to be under the influence of alcohol. When the social worker asks the man if he's been drinking, he replies, "I had three beers today but it was several hours ago." The social worker cancels the man's appointment and asks him to attend the next appointment sober. Canceling this man's appointment:

A) Is an appropriate way to set limits and establish a healthy therapeutic relationship.

B) Is likely to feel punitive to this man and could be very damaging to his treatment goals.

C) Is unwarranted, because the man states he only had three beers, several hours ago, and can still benefit from the session. .

D) Is unethical, because the man is entitled to the appointment.

Answers & Rationales

*Correct answers are in **bold**.*

1. A social worker meets with a 65-year-old woman who reports that she has recently been unable to enter her second bedroom because it is full with her collection of old newspapers and magazines. What diagnosis should the social worker consider FIRST?

Inability to access a room due to an overflow of accumulated possessions is an indicator of possible hoarding disorder. People with hoarding disorder have difficulty discarding their things, often making living areas unusable and experiencing severe distress when it comes to parting with possessions.

   A) Hoarding disorder

   The unusability of living space indicates possible hoarding disorder.

   B) Excoriation disorder

   Excoriation disorder involves recurrent skin picking resulting in skin lesions.

   C) Major depressive disorder

   Decreased energy due to depression can lead to hoarding-like condition, but there are no indicators of MDD in this case.

   D) Obsessive-compulsive disorder

   Hoarding, once categorized as part of OCD, is a separate disorder in DSM-5.

2. The diagnoses autistic disorder, Asperger's disorder, childhood disintegrative disorder, and pervasive developmental disorder NOS are combined into which of the following in DSM-5?

One of the biggest changes in the DSM-5 was the creation of a new diagnosis, autism spectrum disorder, which includes the mentioned diagnoses and allowing for a range of specifiers about severity and presentation.

   A) Neurodevelopmental disorder

   Neurodevelopmental disorders is a DSM-5 chapter containing intellectual disabilities, communication disorders, ADHD, specific learning disorder, and motor disorders, along with autism spectrum disorder.

B) Autism spectrum disorder

> *In DSM-5, the listed diagnoses have been folded into one diagnosis, autism spectrum disorder.*

C) Pervasive development disorder

> *Pervasive developmental disorder is not a diagnosis in DSM-5.*

D) Autistic disorder

> *Autistic disorder is not a DSM-5 diagnosis.*

3. A social worker meets with a 16-year-old boy and his parents. The teenager has recently been expelled from school because of multiple offenses, such as smoking on school property and fighting. The teenager was failing his classes and has an assault charge pending. His parents report feeling their son is depressed. The teenager states he has no problems and no need for meeting with the social worker. What is MOST evident here?

Insight refers to clients' understanding of their illness and their need to seek help. In this instance, the teenager's academic and legal problems point to the need for treatment, so he's clearly lacking insight.

A) The teenager lacks insight.

> *This teenager lacks insight into the seriousness of his problems. His family is concerned about him, he's been expelled from school, he has legal charges pending, and yet he states he doesn't need help.*

B) The teenager has grandiose thoughts.

> *There's no evidence he has grandiose thoughts, which would include believing he's especially important or possesses superhuman abilities.*

C) The teenager has below-average intelligence.

> *The boy's academic failures may be due to a lack of effort or his behavioral problems, so his intelligence may not be an issue.*

D) The teenager is a concrete thinker.

> *There's nothing mentioned that indicates the teenager is a concrete thinker.*

4. A client says to the social worker, "None of my friends like me anymore. I tried to call three of them last night. I left messages but no one called me back. I think they probably all got together and decided they should stop being friends with me." The thoughts the client is having are an example of:

Catastrophic thinking refers to dwelling on worst-case scenarios, without evidence to back them up. People with depression and anxiety are often prone to a variety of catastrophic thoughts.

A) Obsessive thinking

> *Obsessive thinking refers to dwelling on the same thing over and over again, without being able to think about anything else.*

B) Catastrophic thinking

> *This client's conclusion that her friends' lack of response means they no longer like her is an example of catastrophic thinking--imagining the worst-case scenario.*

C) Delusional thinking

> *Delusional thinking refers to holding onto a belief despite clear evidence to the contrary.*

D) Magical thinking

> *Magical thinking refers to the belief that thoughts alone can cause something to happen. For example, a person who wishes his neighbor dead, and blames that thought for the neighbor's getting cancer, is engaging in magical thinking.*

5. It's appropriate to use a provisional diagnosis when:

A provisional diagnosis is appropriate when a social worker doesn't yet have enough information to draw a diagnostic conclusion. Sometimes the client's symptoms may be accounted for by a variety of different diagnoses.

A) A client doesn't quite meet the criteria for a particular diagnosis.

> *If a client doesn't meet the criteria for a diagnosis, the diagnosis should not be given as provisional.*

B) When the social worker is determining whether a client's symptoms stem from substance abuse as opposed to a psychiatric disorder.

> *When it's not yet clear whether the client's symptoms are the result of a mental health issue--rather than substance abuse--it's appropriate to make a provisional diagnosis.*

C) The client's symptoms have not been present for at least three months.

The length of time a person needs to have symptoms present to qualify for a diagnosis varies with each diagnosis.

D) The client doesn't have health insurance, so there's no need for a regular diagnosis.

The diagnosis should not be dependent upon the client's insurance plan.

6. A social worker receives a referral for a person diagnosed with paranoid personality disorder. What is the social worker likely to encounter when working with this person?

People with paranoid personality disorder tend to assume that others have a hidden agenda and will exploit them. They often come across as detached or hostile.

A) Detachment and hostility, since the client is likely to assume the social worker has hidden motives.

People with paranoid personality disorder assume others have secret agendas, and tend to treat social workers with hostility or indifference.

B) An overly dramatic and emotional presentation combined with a need for constant reassurance.

These symptoms are more typical of histrionic personality disorder.

C) Difficulty regulating emotions, thoughts, and impulsive behaviors.

These symptoms are more typical of borderline personality disorder.

D) An inability to recognize social cues and an emotionally cold and indifferent attitude.

These symptoms are more typical of schizoid personality disorder.

7. Dissociative disorders usually stem from:

The various types of dissociative disorders most commonly result from unconscious efforts to cope with childhood trauma.

A) Personality disorders

Personality disorders do not cause dissociative episodes.

B) Physical health issues

Physical health problems are not known to cause dissociative episodes.

C) Anxiety disorders

Anxiety does not usually lead to dissociative episodes.

D) Childhood trauma

Repeated childhood trauma, such as physical or sexual abuse, can lead to dissociative disorders.

8. A social worker meets with a 75-year-old client who is concerned about her recent increase in problems with forgetfulness and confusion. She's says she's not depressed, but can't seem to focus on things as well as she once could. What diagnosis should the social worker first consider?

While she may not yet meet full criteria, the best of the offered diagnoses for the woman is mild neurocognitive decline, which involves a mild decline in cognitive function.

A) Dementia

Dementia is not a diagnosis in DSM-5.

B) Probable vascular neurocognitive disorder

Probable vascular neurocognitive disorder can only be diagnosed with evidence from physical examination and/or neuroimaging.

C) Mild neurocognitive decline

In the absence of depression, the woman's forgetfulness, confusion, and difficulty focusing indicate mild neurocognitive decline.

D) Alzheimer's disease

It is premature to diagnose Alzheimer's disease which involves a gradual, irreversible progression of cognitive impairment. Family history or genetic testing can help clarify if a client has Alzheimer's.

9. A social worker provides consultation to a local preschool program. She notices that a four-year-old boy tends to flinch when approached by adults, and cries when his parents come to pick him up as well. On an occasion when the preschool teacher praises the boy's school behavior, the mother comments that the boy tends to save all his "evil" behavior for home. What is MOST likely indicated here?

Both the child's and the mother's behavior are red flags for physical abuse. When children flinch as adults approach, it can indicate they're abused at home. Although crying when a parent comes to pick up a child isn't necessarily a sign of physical abuse, it often can be, and this mother's comment about the child's "evil" behavior should also raise suspicions. Parents who abuse their children often think of them as being especially bad.

A) The child may be a victim of sexual abuse.

   Typical indicators of sexual abuse include nightmares, bedwetting, difficulty walking, and inappropriate knowledge of sexual activity.

B) The child may be a victim of physical abuse.

   The child's flinching and crying, as well as the mother's comment about his "evil" behavior, are all possible signs of physical abuse.

C) The child likely has some developmental delays.

   There's no evidence this child has developmental delays.

D) The child may be a victim of neglect.

   Warning signs of neglect include a child being inappropriately dressed for the season, begging for money or food, frequent absences from school, and a lack of medical care.

10. A social worker meets with a woman diagnosed with bipolar disorder I. The woman reports that she's been staying in bed much of the time recently, because she feels too depressed to face the day. While she's in bed, she uses her laptop to look for bus tickets to random places where she might move, but her racing thoughts make it difficult for her to follow through with purchasing the tickets. What is MOST likely happening with this woman?

People with bipolar I sometimes experience mixed episodes in which they're depressed and manic at the same time. During a mixed episode, behavior may be erratic, disorganized and rapidly shifting.

A) She's experiencing a depressive episode.

   The fact that this woman is researching random places to move, with accompanying racing thoughts, indicates she may be experiencing mania in addition to her depression.

B) She's experiencing a hypomanic episode.

   Hypomania is characteristic of bipolar II, in which mixed episodes of depression and mania, such as this woman is experiencing, don't typically occur.

C) **She's experiencing a mixed episode.**

   This woman reports simultaneous depression and mania, an indicator of a mixed episode.

D) She's experiencing a manic episode.

   This woman reports she's unable to face the day, so she's likely experiencing depression in addition to her mania.

11. A mother takes her ten-year-old son to see a social worker because the child has not attended school in the past three weeks. The mother states that her son went to school without incident for the first two months, but lately pleads to be allowed to stay home. What is the MOST likely reason for the child's school refusal?

Children who refuse to go to school usually have an underlying anxiety disorder, stemming from peer interactions, the pressures of school work, or separation from caregivers. Treatment for the anxiety often requires exposure therapy and practical problem-solving.

A) Depression

   Although depression can cause children to struggle to find the energy to go to school, consistent school refusal is more often associated with anxiety. Children with depression may oversleep but are less apt to beg to stay home.

B) **Anxiety**

   Anxiety is usually the reason young children attempt to avoid school.

C) Attention deficit hyperactivity disorder

   ADHD is not commonly associated with school refusal.

D) Oppositional defiant disorder

   Since this child was previously attending school without objection, oppositional defiant disorder isn't a likely diagnosis. Children with oppositional defiant disorder will often attend school, but have behavior problems while in school.

12. Delusions of grandeur are most commonly associated with:

Delusions of grandeur are most commonly associated with schizophrenia. They can however, occur with other psychotic disorders and in bipolar disorder. People who have delusions of grandeur may report being in positions of authority or being associated with important people.

A) Mood disorders.

   Although delusions of grandeur can occur with bipolar disorder, they aren't common with other types of depressive disorders.

B) Schizophrenia.

   Delusions of grandeur are most commonly associated with schizophrenia.

C) Histrionic personality disorder.

   People with histrionic personality disorder enjoy being the center of attention, but do not usually exhibit delusions of grandeur.

D) Borderline personality disorder.

   People with borderline personality disorder do not typically report delusions.

13. Adolescents with bipolar I disorder:

Because of the disinhibited behaviors that tend to accompany bipolar I disorder, children and adolescents are more likely to behave in a sexually provocative manner, more willing to try drugs and alcohol, and may therefore be at increased risk for exploitation.

A) May be at increased risk for exploitation due to disinhibited behavior.

   Adolescents with bipolar I are likely to be impulsive and therefore at an increased risk for exploitation.

B) Are likely misdiagnosed because it is rare in young people.

   Bipolar I can be appropriately diagnosed in adolescence and is not a rare occurrence in young people.

C) Do not experience manic episodes.

   Manic episodes must be present for a diagnosis of bipolar I.

D) Are likely to excel in academics because of their increased energy levels.

   Bipolar I is more likely to cause academic impairment.

14. Studies have shown that people with irritable bowel syndrome are likely to suffer from:

Studies have shown that most people with irritable bowel syndrome suffer from anxiety, though it's often unclear whether the anxiety led to the bowel problems or vice versa.

A) Illness anxiety disorder

> *Illness anxiety disorder involves preoccupation with having or acquiring a serious illness and is more. IBS is more likely to be found in people who suffer from GAD.*

B) Somatic symptom disorder

> *Somatic symptom disorder involves symptoms that cannot be explained fully by a general medical condition. People with irritable bowel syndrome are more likely to have an anxiety disorder.*

C) A personality disorder

> *Most people with irritable bowel syndrome have an anxiety disorder.*

D) Generalized anxiety disorder

> *Most people with irritable bowel syndrome tend to worry about a variety of issues, such as money, health, and family.*

15. Which of the following is considered an impulse control disorder?

The DSM-5 chapter, "Disruptive, Impulse-Control, and Conduct Disorders" collects conditions involving problems in the self-control of emotions and behaviors, particularly those in which people are unable to resist performing acts harmful to themselves or others. Impulse-specific disorders from the chapter include kleptomania and pyromania. Disruptive and conduct-specific disorders include oppositional defiant disorder, conduct disorder, and antisocial personality disorder, among others.

A) Kleptomania

> *Kleptomania is considered an impulse control disorder because people suffering from it tend to steal out of temptation and despite potential consequences, not because they need or are unable to pay for the items they're stealing.*

B) Bipolar disorder

> *Although people with bipolar disorder may struggle with impulsivity, especially during manic episodes, it is considered a mood disorder and not an impulse control disorder.*

C) Erotomania

Erotomania is a delusional disorder in which a person feels that someone, usually of higher status, is in love with them.

D) Obsessive-compulsive disorder

Obsessive-compulsive disorder is an anxiety disorder in which people act on obsessive thoughts to relieve their anxiety. Their behavior is not necessarily harmful.

16. A client attends an intake appointment at the social worker's office. The client initially sits down but soon begins walking around the room while answering questions. The client also exhibits handwringing. What is the BEST way for the social worker to describe the observations in the mental status exam?

Psychomotor agitation describes people who exhibit increased motor activity that does not serve any purpose. Pacing and handwringing are common examples.

A) Poor concentration

The client may be able to concentrate on the discussion despite the need to move around.

B) Anxious behavior

The client may not necessarily be anxious. Psychomotor agitation sometimes accompanies schizophrenia or bipolar disorder.

C) Psychomotor retardation

Psychomotor retardation describes a person moving and speaking very slowly.

D) Psychomotor agitation

The client's pacing and handwringing indicate psychomotor agitation.

17. What is the main difference between cyclothymic disorder and bipolar disorder?

People with cyclothymic disorder experience highs and lows, but not with the severity of bipolar disorder. Unlike most people with bipolar disorder, they may experience extended periods of normal mood between the highs and lows, as well as hypomanic episodes with periods of depression too brief to be considered full depressive episodes.

A) People with cyclothymia have more severe mood swings than people with bipolar disorder.

Mood swings are less severe in cyclothymia.

B) People with cyclothymia only experience depressive episodes and do not experience hypomanic episodes.

People with cyclothymia experience hypomanic episodes, which distinguishes cyclothymia from other depressive disorders.

C) People with cyclothymia only experience manic episodes and not depression.

Cyclothymia is characterized by brief depressive episodes as well as periods of hypomania.

D) Mood swings are less severe in cyclothymia than in bipolar disorder.

In cyclothymia, the mood swings are less intense, the depressive episodes are usually brief, and the highs are hypomanic rather than full manic episodes.

18. A man gets scolded by his boss for being late for work. For the rest of the day, he behaves in an especially friendly manner toward his boss, and works through his lunch break. What defense mechanism is this man MOST likely using?

Undoing is a defense mechanism in which people try to nullify behavior that might be considered unacceptable, in this case flattering someone the man offended and working extra hours to make up for lateness.

A) Sublimation

Sublimation refers to channeling unacceptable impulses into more acceptable activities--for example, joking about drinking instead of consuming alcohol.

B) Compartmentalization

Compartmentalization refers to isolating morally contradictory behaviors from each other--for example, behaving honestly at work while cheating on one's taxes.

C) Reaction formation

Reaction formation refers to an overcompensating attitude or behavior opposite to the underlying feeling--for example, acting in an exaggeratedly friendly manner toward a person someone actually hates.

D) Undoing

This man's concerted attempts to atone for being late for work are examples of undoing.

19. A social worker meets with a woman whose relationships tend to last no more than three weeks. Initially, she tells the social worker, she'll describe her new partner as the "best person I've ever met," but within a few weeks tends to say things such as, "He's selfish and doesn't care about how I feel." This type of behavior is MOST common with which diagnosis?

People with borderline personality disorder tend to engage in all-or-nothing thinking, viewing people as either all good or all bad, alternating between idealization and devaluation.

   A) Obsessive compulsive personality disorder

      People with obsessive-compulsive personality disorder are preoccupied with rules, orderliness, and keeping things under control.

   B) Antisocial personality disorder

      People with antisocial personality disorder break laws, violate the rights of others, and indulge in manipulative behavior.

   C) Borderline personality disorder

      This woman views the men in her life as either all good or all bad, a common feature of borderline personality disorder.

   D) Dependent personality disorder

      People with dependent personality disorder have an extreme fear of abandonment, seek to remain in relationships, and tend to appear "clingy."

20. Common symptoms of paranoid personality disorder include:

People with paranoid personality disorder tend to presume that everyone is out to get them. They are suspicious of everyone, including friends and family and often report finding hidden meaning behind a person's body language or conversation. They tend to hold grudges and lack trust in others.

   A) Rapidly shifting shallow expression of emotions.

      Rapidly shifting and shallow expression of emotions is more indicative of histrionic personality disorder. People with paranoid personality tend not to show much emotion, with the exception of anger.

   B) Persistent belief that a lover is cheating.

      Many people with paranoid personality disorder firmly believe that a spouse or lover is cheating on them, despite a lack of evidence.

C) Auditory and visual hallucinations.

> *People with paranoid personality disorder tend to hold onto delusional beliefs but don't usually report hallucinations.*

D) Hoarding objects with little or no monetary value.

> *Hoarding is a symptom of hoarding disorder, not paranoid personality disorder.*

21. A school social worker receives a referral from the physical education teacher. A ten-year-old girl has started refusing to change her clothes in the locker room with the other girls. This behavior may be a symptom of:

A child's refusal to participate in physical activity or change in front of peers can be an indicator of sexual abuse.

A) Conduct disorder

> *Although it may appear this child is being defiant, a diagnosis of conduct order is unlikely, unless the child is exhibiting other behavioral issues.*

B) Sexual abuse

> *A refusal to change clothes and participate in physical is a possible sign of sexual abuse.*

C) Neglect

> *A refusal to change clothes for physical education is not a sign of neglect. Frequent absences from school, begging for or stealing food or money, a lack of appropriate clothing or medical care, are the typical indicators of neglect.*

D) ADHD

> *A refusal to change clothing in front of peers is not usually indicative of ADHD.*

22. Which of the following comorbidities is the most common with ADHD?

Most children with ADHD have at least one comorbidity, including conduct disorder, anxiety, depression, speech problems, and, most commonly, learning disorders.

A) Bipolar disorder

> *It's possible for children to have both ADHD and bipolar disorder, but it's less common than other comorbidities.*

B) Sleeping disorders

Although some children with ADHD have difficulty sleeping, it's a less common comorbidity than learning disability.

C) Eating disorders

Most children with ADHD have a learning disability, not an eating disorder.

D) Learning disorders

Most children with ADHD have a learning disability.

23. A college student meets with a social worker because he has a problem with numbers. He states that he needs things to end on an even number; if class ends at 45 minutes past the hour, he won't get up from seat until the clock shows 46 minutes. He states that odd numbers are "bad" and he fears something bad will happen if he ignores them. What is the MOST likely diagnosis?

Since the client is having unwanted obsessive thoughts (that odd numbers are bad) leading to compulsive behavior (inability to leave class until the clock shows an even number), he's experiencing definitive symptoms of OCD.

A) Schizophrenia

The client's obsessive thoughts are indicative of OCD, not schizophrenia.

B) Obsessive-compulsive disorder

This client's obsessive thoughts and compulsive behavior are consistent with OCD.

C) Specific phobia

This client's anxiety seems related to his obsessive thoughts, an indicator of OCD.

D) Delusional disorder

There's evidence of obsession, not delusion here. OCD is the more likely diagnosis..

24. Which of the following treatments is an example of aversion therapy to treat alcohol addiction?

Aversion therapy is a form of classical conditioning that leads to behavioral change. In cases of alcoholism, Antabuse is sometimes used to cause people to feel nauseated when they drink, and therefore cut down their cravings for alcohol.

A) Alcoholics Anonymous

Alcoholics Anonymous is a supportive treatment that helps people manage their addiction, but does not involve inducing adverse reactions to alcohol.

B) Antabuse

Antabuse is a drug that causes people to feel ill if they drink alcohol, thereby reducing their cravings for alcohol by associating drinking with nausea.

C) Methadone

Methadone assists people withdrawing from opioids.

D) Electroconvulsive therapy

Electroconvulsive therapy induces seizures and is sometimes used to treat depression or schizophrenia.

25. The main difference between schizophrenia and schizophreniform disorder is:

Schizophreniform disorder is the appropriate diagnosis when symptoms have lasted six months or less. When symptoms persist beyond six months, the diagnosis should change to schizophrenia.

A) Schizophreniform disorder includes abnormal moods in addition to psychosis, while schizophrenia doesn't involve abnormal moods.

Mood issues combined with psychotic features are characteristic of schizoaffective disorder.

B) Schizophreniform disorder includes a lack of interest in social relationships while people with schizophrenia enjoy social relationships.

A lack of interest in social relationships is characteristic of schizoid personality disorder.

C) In schizophreniform disorder, the symptoms have lasted less than six months; in schizophrenia, the symptoms have lasted six months or more.

In schizophreniform disorder, symptoms last six months or less. Schizophrenia is a lifelong illness.

D) Schizophrenia is more typical in adults while schizophreniform disorder occurs during adolescence.

Both schizophrenia and schizophreniform disorder usually begin during late adolescence or young adulthood.

26. A social worker in an outpatient mental health clinic meets with a new client. What is the BEST way to determine a client's level of judgment?

A "What would you do if..." question is a good way to determine a client's level of judgment, including the ability to make a healthy choice.

A) Ask the client to explain the meaning of a proverb such as, "A rolling stone gathers no moss."

Asking a client to explain a proverb would help the social worker gain insight into the client's ability to think abstractly.

B) Ask the client a question, such as "What would you do if you found a pair of car keys sitting on the ground in the parking lot of a grocery store?"

Whether the client, in answering the question, steps over the keys, keeps them or turns them over to an employee, will help the social worker determine the client's ability to make a good choice.

C) Ask the client directly whether or not he thinks he has good judgment.

Many people with judgment issues are unaware they have poor judgment.

D) Ask the client to memorize four objects and recall those objects after five minutes.

Asking the client to repeat objects he's memorized will only offer insight into his memory.

27. A client tells a social worker, "I feel so frustrated that my husband doesn't help around the house. He says he works too hard at his job to come home and do any cleaning." Which of the following responses is the BEST example of active listening?

Active listening requires the social worker to show a genuine interest in and understanding of what the client is saying, clearly reflecting back the facts or feelings the client is conveying.

A) "Should we discuss how your resentment is likely to lead to other problems in your relationship?"

Suggesting it's time to draw conclusions doesn't show the client the social worker fully understands what the client is trying to convey.

B) "You feel angry that you have to bear all of the responsibility at home."

The client hasn't said she's angry with her husband, nor that she bears any household responsibilities other than household chores.

C) "Your husband believes men should be the breadwinners and shouldn't have to do household chores."

The client hasn't stated he thinks no men should have to do household chores, just that he works too hard at his job to be expected to help with the cleaning.

D) "You feel frustrated that your husband doesn't feel he should have to help out around the house."

This response reflects back the same feeling word the client used, as well as the facts the client stated.

28. During an intake assessment, a social worker asks a client to memorize four unrelated objects, then moves on to other questions. Five minutes later, the social worker asks the client to recall those four objects. What information is the social worker MOST LIKELY trying to obtain?

Assessing a client's memory is an important part of a mental status exam. Asking a client to memorize something and then recall it several minutes later is a valid test of a client's short-term memory.

A) The social worker wants to assess the client's intelligence.

Asking a client to memorize and recall objects is not a good measure of intelligence.

B) The social worker wants to examine the client's short-term memory.

Asking the client to remember objects that were memorized a few minutes before is a good measure of short-term memory.

C) The social worker wants to examine the client's remote memory.

Remote memory refers to memory of events from six months ago and longer; short-term memory refers to events over the past two hours.

D) The social worker is attempting to examine the client's ability to manage stress.

> *Since a memory test may not be stressful to everyone, this task may not accurately measure a client's coping abilities.*

29. A social worker at a community mental health center is meeting with a client for the first time. The social worker wants to test the client's abstract thinking. What question would BEST evaluate the client's ability to think abstractly?

Asking clients how two objects are alike or how they are similar is a way to assess their abstract thinking abilities--their capacity to grasp intangibles and respond to questions that don't have right or wrong answers. Offering a proverb to decipher is another strategy.

A) How are dogs and cats alike?

> *Since this question has multiple answers and requires a level of abstract thought, it's an appropriate question to ask to assess abstract thinking ability.*

B) Can you name the last four presidents of the United States?

> *Since the answer to this question is concrete, it doesn't test abstract thinking abilities.*

C) Have you ever felt your mind was playing tricks on you?

> *Asking if a person's mind has ever played tricks on them may help determine a history of psychosis, but doesn't test abstract thinking.*

D) Who is the president of the United States?

> *This question has a concrete answer, and doesn't help evaluate a client's ability to think abstractly.*

30. A mother takes her four-year-old daughter to meet with a social worker. The mother says the family experienced a house fire, and though everyone got out safely, she thinks her daughter may be traumatized as a result. The family is now staying with the mother's parents until they can rebuild. What would be the BEST question to determine if the child might have PTSD?

Young children who aren't able to verbalize their anxiety will often engage in traumatic play if they are experiencing symptoms of PTSD. Traumatic play is often repetitive and involves replaying and acting out the trauma.

A) Ask the child if she likes living with her grandparents.

> *The child's opinion about living with her grandparents does not help with diagnosing PTSD.*

B) Ask the child if she worries about fires.

> *This is a leading question likely to evoke a simple yes or no answer, and won't help determine if the child has any symptoms.*

C) Ask the mother if the child is adjusting to the new living situation.

> *This child's adjustment to her new living situation is a separate issue from PTSD. She could be adjusting well and still have PTSD.*

D) Ask the mother if the child engages in repeated play reenacting the fire.

> *Since this child is only four years old and has experienced a trauma, it's important to know how much of her play centers on the fire. Trauma-themed play can be a symptom of PTSD.*

31. A social worker is conducting an initial assessment on a woman who has decided to seek help for her grief. As the woman describes her brother's murder, she smiles and laughs throughout the account. What should the social worker note in the mental status exam?

When people express their emotions in a way that doesn't match what they're saying, they're exhibiting inappropriate affect. This woman is discussing her brother's murder, so her laughter is an inappropriate expression of her emotions.

A) Euthymic affect

> *Euthymic affect refers to a reasonably positive mood congruent to the subject at hand.*

B) Flat affect

> *A flat affect refers to a lack of expression or monotone.*

C) Blunted affect

> *Blunted affect refers to a significant reduction in a person's emotional expression*

D) Inappropriate affect

> *Inappropriate affect refers to a discrepancy between the subject matter that's being discussed and the emotion that's expressed.*

32. A social worker in a community mental health center meets with an eight-year-old child and his grandmother to conduct a biopsychosocial assessment. The child was recently placed with his grandmother by child protective services because of his mother's substance-abuse problem. During the initial interview, the grandmother focuses on the mother's long-term heavy drinking, and states she doesn't think the mother will ever be able to get the child back. When the social worker asks about the child's background and history, the grandmother continues to focus on the mother's drinking. What is the BEST way for the social worker to proceed?

As a rule, social workers in community mental health centers need to formulate a diagnosis by the end of a session. For a thorough biopsychosocial assessment to be productive, clients should be made aware of the purpose of the interview, and the social worker should remain in charge of the interview process.

A) The social worker should ask the grandmother to leave the session and interview the child alone.

   Since an eight-year-old isn't likely to have the information needed for a diagnosis and an intervention strategy, interviewing the child isn't apt to be helpful.

B) The social worker should stop asking questions and let the grandmother use the session to discuss her concerns.

   The social worker should remain in control of the interview, in order to gather information that will lead to a diagnosis and an intervention strategy.

C) The social worker should focus the interview on what the grandmother wants to discuss by asking more questions about the mother's drinking.

   To complete a thorough assessment, the social worker will need other information about the child, not just the grandmother's views on the mother's drinking.

D) The social worker should underscore the purpose for gathering background information and continue asking questions.

   The social worker should help the grandmother understand the purpose of discussing topics other than the mother's drinking, and remain in charge of the interview process.

33. A busy primary care practice employs ten doctors and two social workers. The doctors have noticed that many of their patients with somatic complaints actually have underlying depression, but don't always have time to assess a person's mental health and then refer them for social work services during the appointment. What is the BEST way for the office to identify depressed patients who may benefit from social work services?

Many people with depression report physical health symptoms which lead them to consult their primary care doctor, who may or may not identify the underlying depression during an appointment. Screening tools can be the quickest way for physicians to identify these patients, who can then be referred to social work services.

A) Posters should be placed in the lobby encouraging patients to ask for a social work referral if they're depressed.

> *Many patients don't know when they're depressed, so a poster isn't likely to encourage them to seek help.*

B) All patients could be given a depression screening to help identify those who may be suffering from depression.

> *A screening tool can be the fastest and most cost-effective way for physicians to identify patients who need a social work referral.*

C) The reception staff should begin asking patients if they'd like to speak with a social worker.

> *Patients don't always know how social workers can be helpful, so having the reception staff ask if patients want to see a social worker is inappropriate.*

D) The office should hire more social workers, so that each patient can be interviewed about possible symptoms of depression.

> *Hiring enough social workers to interview every single patient isn't likely to be feasible.*

34. The difference between a screening and an assessment is:

Screening is a process for evaluating the possible presence of a problem, such as a developmental delay, mental health problem or substance abuse issue. Screenings often involve yes or no questions. If a screening indicates there may be a problem, an assessment can be conducted to determine if in fact a problem exists, how to address the problem and how to diagnose the problem.

A) A screening requires specialized training and expertise and an assessment is used to determine a diagnosis.

> *Most screening tools do not require specialized training or expertise.*

B) An assessment usually consists of yes or no questions and a screening defines the extent of the problem.

> *A screening usually consists of yes or no questions while an assessment tends to involve open ended interview questions that can determine the extent of the problem.*

C) A screening determines the diagnosis and the assessment establishes recommendations to address the problem.

> *A screening does not establish the diagnosis. Instead, it can help determine if further assessment is needed.*

D) **A screening evaluates the possible presence of a problem and an assessment defines the nature of a problem.**

> *Screening tools identify the presence of possible problems and often involve yes or no questions. An assessment can determine a diagnosis, treatment recommendations and the extent of the problem.*

35. A social worker conducting an initial assessment asks the client if she's ever driven to perform behaviors as a result of repeated, unwanted thoughts. What is the social worker MOST likely to trying to learn?

Repeated hand-washing, checking things over and over, or putting things in a certain order for no good reason, are all examples of compulsive behaviors. When these behaviors are driven by obsessive thoughts, it may indicate obsessive-compulsive disorder. For example, a woman who has constant thoughts about germs may exhibit compulsive hand-washing to reduce her anxiety.

A) The social worker wants to know if the woman is autistic.

> *Although repetitive behaviors can be common in autism spectrum disorder, they're not likely caused by intrusive thoughts.*

B) The social worker wants to know if the woman has a specific phobia.

> *Specific phobias do not cause repetitive behaviors.*

C) The social worker wants to know if the woman has flashbacks, such as those found in PTSD.

> *Although flashbacks can cause intrusive thoughts, they don't usually lead to repetitive behaviors.*

D) **The social worker wants to know if the woman has any compulsions, such as those found in OCD.**

> *Asking about repetitive behaviors is appropriate to assess whether a client has OCD.*

36. A social worker receives a referral from child protective services for a 35-year-old woman. Child protective services removed the woman's children from her care because they had evidence that the woman's boyfriend was sexually abusing the children. When the social worker meets with the woman for the initial assessment, how should the social worker use the information received from child protective services?

If a social worker has received information about clients from another source, the social worker should be upfront and honest about the information, and ask open-ended questions to encourage clients to tell the story in their own words.

A) The social worker should neither read the reports nor acknowledge receiving them.

> *Since the woman was referred by child protective services, and the information could be helpful in treatment, the social worker should read the reports.*

B) The social worker should give the reports to the woman to read so she can say what is true and what isn't.

> *The decision to release the information to the woman is up to child protective services and not the social worker.*

C) The social worker should tell the woman the reports have been received and ask her to tell the story from her point of view.

> *Acknowledging that the social worker already has information about the client, and then inviting the woman to tell her story in her own words, is the appropriate course.*

D) The social worker should read the reports but not let the woman know the information was received.

> *The social worker should be honest about receiving information from other sources.*

37. A college student meets with a social worker on campus. The student states she has difficulty paying attention during class, is easily distracted when doing homework, has trouble staying organized, and loses items frequently. What question would MOST help the social worker determine if the student might have ADHD?

In order for a person to meet the diagnostic criteria for ADHD, symptoms must be present for at least six months.

A) Are you hyperactive?

> *Hyperactivity is not required for a diagnosis of ADHD. Problems with attention alone are sufficient to meet criteria.*

B) How often do you drink alcohol?

Although it's important to ask clients about their substance use, a client's drinking behavior is not going to rule in or rule out ADHD.

C) How long have you been experiencing these problems?

Symptoms of ADHD must be present for a minimum of six months before a diagnosis can be made.

D) Do you have difficulty sleeping?

Sleep issues are not associated with ADHD.

38. A school social worker meets with a 14-year-old boy. The boy states that several nights ago he and some other boys spray-painted graffiti on the side of a building. Upon learning this information, what obligation does the social worker have?

Unless the information clients disclose is related to child abuse or places someone in imminent danger, social workers must maintain confidentiality.

A) The social worker is obligated to report the crime to the police department.

Social workers are not obligated to report crimes to the police.

B) The social worker is obligated to notify the teen's parents.

The social worker needs to keep the information confidential.

C) The social worker is obligated to keep the information confidential.

The social worker needs to maintain confidentiality.

D) The social worker is obligated to notify the school of the incident.

Notifying the school would be a breach of confidentiality.

39. A 15-year-old boy tells a social worker he thinks most of his problems started when his stepfather came into his life. He states he sometimes fantasizes about murdering his stepfather, but denies having a plan to kill him. How should the social worker respond?

Social workers should maintain confidentiality except for select circumstances. Since this child doesn't seem to have any serious intent to kill his stepfather, the social worker shouldn't break confidentiality.

A) The social worker should make a report to child protective services.

There's no indication of child abuse, so there's no need to make a child protective report.

B) The social worker should maintain the client's confidentiality.

Since there's no sign of imminent risk, the proper response is to maintain confidentiality.

C) The social worker has a duty to warn the stepfather.

There's nothing to indicate the stepfather is in imminent danger, so there's no duty to warn.

D) The social worker should tell the boy's mother.

The social worker should only tell the client's mother if the child agrees to it.

40. A social worker has been meeting with a woman who is experiencing stress as a single parent. During a regularly scheduled appointment, the woman acknowledges slapping her daughter across the face and hitting her son with a belt. She states she is very sorry and is certain she will not do this again. How should the social worker handle this?

Child abuse and neglect need to be reported to child protective services, even when parents acknowledge the abuse and are working on it in treatment.

A) Inform the woman of the obligation to report the incident to child protective services and continue to work with her on ways to reduce her stress.

It's appropriate to inform the woman that a report will be made and to continue to work with her on her treatment goals.

B) Since the woman has acknowledged the abuse, the abuse is now a treatment issue, and there's no need to report it to child protective services.

Even if the woman is working on this issue in treatment, it still needs to be reported to child protective services.

C) Make a call to child protective services without telling the woman, since disclosure may damage the therapeutic relationship and discourage the woman from seeking further help.

While the social worker must contact child protective services about the abuse, it's also important to be up front with the client about making the report. If the woman finds out the social worker has made the report behind her back, the therapeutic relationship may be seriously compromised.

D) Contact the children's guidance counselor at school and request the children be interviewed to see what their side of the story is.

   Talking to the school would be a non-mandated breach in confidentiality.

41. A social worker is seeing a client who has just been charged with murder. The social worker is contacted by a reporter who wants to know whether or not the client has a mental illness. The reporter states that he contacted the client in jail and the client confirmed that he sees the social worker for treatment. How should the social worker respond?

The NASW Code of Ethics is clear that social workers need to protect client confidentiality, with very few exceptions. If social workers are contacted by members of the media, the social worker should not even confirm knowing the client.

A) The social worker should decline to confirm whether or not the person is a client.

   It would be a breach of confidentiality to give any information that confirms the client is known to the social worker.

B) The social worker should tell the reporter that the client will need to sign a release of information prior to any discussion.

   Telling the reporter that a release will need to be obtained implies that the social worker does in fact see the client--a violation of confidentiality.

C) The social worker can confirm that the client has been in treatment but should not offer any details.

   It would be a breach of confidentiality to reveal that the person is the social worker's client.

D) Since it's a public safety issue, the social worker has the discretion to disclose information about the client's treatment.

   Since the client is in jail, there's no likely threat to public safety. The social worker should reveal no information whatsoever, including knowledge of the client.

42. According to HIPAA, communicating with clients via email and sending information to other agencies via fax is:

HIPAA outlines security measures that health agencies and certain businesses must follow to protect a client's health information. According to HIPAA, electronic communication is allowable, but social workers should take steps to reduce the risk of breaching confidentiality.

A) Only allowable for non-identifiable information.

Social workers may send confidential information via fax or email as long as there are certain safeguards in place.

B) **Allowable with certain safeguards in place.**

It's allowable to use certain forms of electronic communication as long as there are protective measures in place to reduce the risk of breaching confidentiality.

C) Never allowed.

Electronic communication is permitted if certain safeguards are in place.

D) Always allowed.

Electronic forms of communication are allowable only when social workers take steps to reduce the risk of breaching confidentiality.

43. A social worker has been in private practice for ten years. The social worker shares office space with two other social workers and two receptionists. What is the BEST way for the social worker to store the files of clients who have been discharged?

Social workers should keep inactive files safely locked away for the duration required by state law, at minimum. Records should be inaccessible to reception staff, other social workers, and other office personnel.

A) The social worker should keep the records where the office staff and other social workers in the building can have access if necessary.

These are confidential records, and no one else's access is necessary.

B) **The social worker should keep the files locked up in a place where no one else will have access.**

When a social worker is in private practice, it's appropriate to keep inactive files locked up, inaccessible to other office staff.

C) Social workers should ship old records to a third-party storage agency.

Sending records to a third party leaves the social worker unable to assure confidentiality.

D) Since inactive files should be purged one year after discharge, the social worker shouldn't be storing old records.

Social workers should store old records in the event that clients request them.

44. A school social worker receives a referral for an eight-year-old girl who is very disruptive in class. After a couple of months of weekly meetings, the girl discloses that her uncle, who often visits the home, has been sexually abusing her for about a year. Who should be made aware of this disclosure?

Social workers are mandated reporters of child abuse and neglect. If a child discloses abuse, social workers should notify child protective services, and, when appropriate to do so, the parents, to help them keep the child safe.

A) Child protective services only

The parents should be notified in addition to child protective services so that the parents can help protect the child from her uncle.

B) Child protective services and the child's parents

It's appropriate to make a mandated report to child protective services, and to notify the parents so they can protect this child from her uncle.

C) Child protective services, the teacher who referred the child, and the child's parents

School personnel should not be informed of the child's disclosure.

D) Child protective services and the school department

The school department should not be informed of the child's disclosure.

45. A social worker is providing outpatient substance-abuse services to a woman who has been diagnosed with alcohol abuse. The woman reports that one night last week while she was drinking, her six-year-old daughter tried to dump her alcohol down the drain. The client states that she slammed her daughter's head into the floor repeatedly out of anger. The woman states she would have never done anything like this sober, she's stopped drinking, and swears she'll never drink again. How should the social worker respond?

Although people with substance-abuse problems are afforded extra confidentiality, social workers are still mandated reporters of child abuse and neglect. If a person with a substance-abuse problem places a child in danger, a report needs to be made.

A) The social worker must make a mandatory report to child protective services.

Since the woman has physically abused her child, the social worker is required to make a report to child protective services.

B) The social worker should refrain from making a report, because the woman is being treated for substance abuse, which allows this woman a higher level of confidentiality.

Even though the client has a substance-abuse diagnosis, the social worker is still mandated to make a report to child protective services.

C) The social worker should document the incident, and if it happens again, make a report to child protective services.

The social worker should both document the incident and make the report, rather than wait until the next time the child is abused.

D) Since the woman states she's stopped drinking, the social worker doesn't need to make a report to child protective services.

Even if this woman states she stopped drinking, she may drink again, and in any event case a report of child abuse is mandated.

46. A social worker conducts couples therapy with a husband and wife. After several sessions, the couple separate. The social worker receives a request from the man's attorney for the social worker's treatment records. The man has signed a release of information for any and all records. What should the social worker do FIRST?

In working with couples, social workers should protect confidentiality of both parties, including when a divorce or separation occurs. Court proceedings can become complicated, and social workers should seek legal consultation.

A) The social worker should call the wife and ask if she wants the records released.

Rather than call the woman and reveal that the man has signed a release of information, the social worker should seek legal consultation before proceeding.

B) The social worker should release records to both the husband and wife and not give them to a third party.

Rather than release the records to both parties--a potentially damaging course--the social worker should seek legal counsel.

C) The social worker should provide all the records when asked to do so.

Since only one party has authorized release of the records, the social worker should maintain confidentiality for both parties, and seek legal counsel.

D) The social worker should seek legal consultation about how to proceed.

The social worker should seek legal consultation to find out how to proceed, given the obligation to maintain confidentiality for both parties.

47. A social worker receives an invitation to a surprise birthday party for a friend. The party will be held at one of the social worker's client's homes. How should the social worker respond to the invitation?

Social workers should respect a client's right to privacy. This entails not only keeping information from the sessions confidential, but also taking care not to reveal when a person is a client. Social workers should also avoid dual relationships with clients.

A) The social worker should talk with the client about the awkward situation and ask that the party be moved somewhere else.

Since it's a therapist's responsibility to maintain boundaries, asking the client to move the party would be inappropriate.

B) The social worker should attend the party because not attending may hurt the client's feelings.

If accepting the invitation risks revealing that the host is a client, the social worker should not attend the party.

C) The social worker should decline the invitation by saying there is a conflict of interest, without stating the precise nature of the conflict.

If the social worker reveals there's a conflict of interest, the other guests may infer that the host is the social worker's client, which amounts to a breach of confidentiality.

D) The social worker should decline the invitation without revealing that the host is a client.

The social worker should decline the invitation, taking care not to reveal the reason, since that would constitute a breach of the therapeutic relationship.

48. A social worker has been working with a woman for several months. The woman has an upcoming court date to address custody issues regarding her child. The social worker receives a call from the woman's lawyer, who wants the social worker's opinion about this woman's ability to successfully parent her child. The social worker should FIRST:

Social workers should not talk to a client's attorney without written permission from the client. When it comes to confidentiality, a client's lawyer should be treated like any other outside person or agency.

A) Tell the lawyer that nothing will be discussed until a subpoena is received.

> *The social worker can talk to the client's lawyer without a subpoena, but a release of information must first be obtained.*

B) Provide written copies of the woman's treatment goals.

> *Before the social worker can discuss the client with the lawyer, the client needs to sign a release of information.*

C) Obtain a release of information from the woman before talking to the lawyer.

> *The social worker needs written permission from the client to release any information to the lawyer.*

D) Discuss only facts with the lawyer, and not offer any opinions.

> *The social worker needs a release of information from the client before any information can be discussed.*

49. A social worker meets with a woman for an initial assessment. The woman reports symptoms of depression that began recently, and states she was married twice. When the social worker asks about those marriages, the woman says she doesn't want to talk about them. How should the social worker proceed?

If clients don't wish to talk about certain topics, the Code of Ethics is clear that social workers should respect their right to privacy, and should refrain from asking questions that aren't directly related to the treatment.

A) In order to encourage the client to talk about her marriages, the social worker should explain the importance of discussing past relationships.

> *If the client doesn't wish to discuss something from her past, the social worker shouldn't press the issue, particularly if the subject isn't necessarily related to her treatment.*

B) **Since the woman's past relationships aren't likely to be related to her current depression, the social worker should respect her right to privacy and not ask any further questions.**

> *The social worker should respect the client's wishes, which are consistent with her right to privacy.*

C) The social worker should end the interview and tell the woman she can resume when she feels ready to talk.

> *Rather than discontinue treatment, the social worker should respect the client's right to privacy.*

D) The social worker should tell the woman that without a thorough assessment, it's unlikely her depression can be treated successfully.

> *Since the woman states her symptoms began recently, the social worker doesn't need the details of her past relationships in order to conduct a thorough assessment.*

50. A social worker met with a woman who shared some recent suicidal ideation. The client refused to go to the emergency room, and the social worker allowed her to return home. The social worker is uncertain whether she did the right thing, and chooses to consult a colleague about the incident. In terms of revealing the client's name, what should the social worker do?

Unless revealing a client's name may prevent harm to self or others, social workers should refrain from revealing identifying information to a colleague when consulting them for an opinion.

A) The social worker should reveal the client's name so they can both document that the social worker sought consultation.

> *The social worker and the colleague can document that the social worker sought consultation without the colleague's knowing the client's name.*

B) The social worker can reveal the client's name only if the colleague works for the same agency.

> *Even if the colleague works for the same agency, a social worker should not reveal private information about clients.*

C) **The social worker should not reveal the client's name or any identifying information about the client.**

> *The social worker should maintain confidentiality and refrain from giving any identifying information about the client.*

D) It is acceptable to reveal the client's name to a colleague since it involves a safety issue.

Though the client is at risk for suicide, there's no need to reveal the client's name to the colleague.

51. When a social worker provides clinical supervision to another social worker, what is the supervisor's liability?

Clinical supervisors have the responsibility to offer recommendations to a supervisee that encourage ethical conduct. If a supervisor is negligent or does not make appropriate recommendations, the supervisor can be held liable.

A) A supervisor who doesn't have direct contact with the client doesn't have any liability.

Even if a clinical supervisor doesn't have direct client contact, the supervisor can be held liable for improper supervision.

B) A clinical supervisor can be held liable for inadequate or negligent supervision.

A supervisor can be held liable if supervision is deemed inadequate or inappropriate.

C) A clinical supervisor only has liability if the supervisor is also the agency supervisor.

A clinical supervisor doesn't need to be the agency supervisor in order to be held liable.

D) Supervisors can only be sued by the supervisee and cannot be held liable by the client.

Supervisors can be held liable by a client, an agency or by the supervisee.

52. A social worker conducts an assessment on a man with a substance-abuse problem. The social worker doesn't have expertise in substance abuse and feels the client will be best served by being transferred to someone else. The social worker is aware of two social workers in the area who do substance-abuse treatment, one of whom the social worker has worked closely with and whose expertise the social worker especially trusts. How should the social worker proceed when giving information about referral options?

When social workers make referrals, they should offer at least two choices, and encourage clients to do their own research on which option sounds like the best match.

A) The social worker should recommend the client find someone with substance-abuse expertise, but not offer any names.

Leaving the client to fend for himself is a form of abandonment, so the social worker should offer the names of people with more expertise--but without revealing a preference.

B) The social worker should offer only the name of the person the social worker especially trusts.

When referring clients, social workers should offer the names of at least two different agencies or social workers.

C) The social worker should offer both names, but discuss why the social worker prefers one over the other.

The social worker should offer both names, but remain neutral.

D) The social worker should offer the client the names of the two social workers, and remain neutral about both.

The social worker should allow the client to choose between the two social workers, and refrain from showing any special preference.

53. A social worker has been meeting with a self-referred man who has a history of depression and alcoholism. Besides addressing his substance abuse and mental health with the social worker, the man attends AA meetings, and sees a counselor mandated by his probation. In terms of collaboration, what is the MOST important thing the social worker should do?

Social workers who work with people with substance abuse often need to collaborate with other professionals. It's the social worker's responsibility to make sure the client's needs are being met through the other services, and that services aren't being duplicated.

A) The social worker should consult with the client's probation officer to see what sort of counseling the man is receiving.

Although the social worker may contact the probation officer, it's best to contact the other counselor directly, since the probation officer won't likely know the extent of the counseling goals and treatment.

B) The social worker should consult with the client's insurance company to ensure that services aren't being duplicated.

Although it can be helpful to make sure services are covered by insurance, insurance companies may have a different view of what constitutes duplicate services.

C) **The social worker should consult with the other counselor to ensure that services are not being duplicated.**

> *Since duplicate services can create billing issues, waste the time of both social worker and client, and cause other confusions, the social worker should contact the counselor directly to see if services are in fact being duplicated.*

D) The social worker does not need to collaborate with other professionals, since the client's other counseling is part of a court order.

> *It's important to collaborate with the other counselor to ensure that services are not being duplicated.*

54. A social worker receives a referral for a client whose employee assistance program only allows for three therapy sessions. In addition to lacking health insurance and other financial issues, the client has a lengthy history of trauma, is currently going through a divorce, and is having problems at work. The social worker tends to use art therapy and narrative therapy as principal treatment modalities. What is the BEST way for the social worker to proceed?

If a social worker doesn't have expertise in a particular type of treatment, it's important to transfer the client to someone who does-- especially if the social worker uses long-term therapies and the client's limited coverage only permits short-term solutions.

A) The social worker should treat the client the same way that anyone with health insurance would be treated.

> *Offering treatment in the normal fashion for a client who only has coverage for three sessions may not give the client an opportunity to resolve her issues.*

B) The social worker should warn the client prior to her first session that she will most likely need long-term therapy and may have to pay out of pocket.

> *Since this woman has financial problems, it's unlikely she'll be able to afford the social worker's services, which utilize long-term therapies. A transfer to a social worker with expertise in short-term counseling is indicated.*

C) **The social worker should refer the woman to someone who has expertise in solution-focused or other short-term therapies.**

> *In view of this woman's limited coverage, referring her to someone with expertise in short-term therapy is the appropriate course.*

D) The social worker should try to do her usual treatment in three sessions.

> *Attempting to use long-term therapies in a very limited amount of time isn't likely to be effective.*

55. A 25-year-old man meets with a social worker because he is embarrassed by his premature ejaculation. He is in a fairly new but serious relationship and thinks it is impacting their love life. What is the FIRST thing the social worker should do?

Health issues, such as thyroid problems or hormonal imbalances, are among the many possible causes of premature ejaculation. A social worker should recommend a client have a complete physical health examination prior to addressing the problem from a psychological or relational standpoint.

A) Instruct him on the "squeeze technique" to help him learn to delay orgasm.

   The squeeze technique is a common way to help men delay ejaculation, but it is first important to rule out physical health problems.

B) Refer him to a sex therapist, especially if the social worker lacks expertise in this area.

   A client should first be referred to a primary care physician to rule out physical health issues. If the social worker does not have expertise in this area, a later referral to a specialist may be appropriate.

C) Recommend he meet with his primary care physician to rule out any biological causes.

   It is appropriate to refer this man to his primary care physician to ensure health problems aren't contributing to his premature ejaculation. Once physical issues have been ruled out, the social worker can address the other possible causes and treatments.

D) Recommend his partner attend treatment with him, since this issue is best dealt with as a couple.

   It's important to first rule out physical causes. Then, depending on the circumstances, it may or may not be appropriate to deal with the issue as a couple.

56. A clinical social worker has been in practice for seven years. The social worker works full-time at a community mental health center. As part of best practice, how much supervision should the social worker receive?

Supervision is important for social workers throughout their careers, especially newer social workers. State licensing boards, malpractice insurers and third party reimbursement agencies sometimes have requirements about how much supervision a social worker should receive. A clinical social worker with several years of experience should establish supervision on an "as needed" basis—weekly or less frequently, depending on the individual.

A) The social worker should receive supervision on an "as needed" basis.

It's appropriate for a social worker with several years of experience to determine how much supervision is required.

B) The social worker should receive one hour of supervision for every 18 hours of direct service work.

For advanced social workers, the number of hours of supervision will vary depending on the social worker's needs.

C) After seven years of clinical practice, the social worker does not need any supervision.

It is best practice for social workers to receive some form of supervision.

D) The social worker should receive one hour per week of supervision.

The number of hours of supervision will vary depending on the needs of the social worker.

57. A social worker consults with a supervisor after a particularly difficult session with a client. The supervisor suggests the social worker begin doing process recordings with the client. Which of the following is the supervisor specifically recommending?

Process recordings, a helpful teaching tool, involve writing down word for word as much as the social worker can recall from the session, including the social worker's feelings, and then reviewing the session with the supervisor.

A) Use a two-way mirror so other social workers can observe the sessions.

Process recordings do not involve the use of a two-way mirror.

B) After each session write down word for word everything the social worker can recall.

Process recordings involve writing down everything the social can recall from the session, word for word if possible, along with the social worker's feelings.

C) Bring a tape recorder to each session with the client and record what is said.

Process recordings do not require the use of an audio recording.

D) Videotape each session, with the client's permission.

Process recordings do not involve video tapes.

58. When a social worker meets with a clinical supervisor, what are the recommendations regarding documentation?

It's important for a supervisor and the supervisee to document the frequency and duration of clinical supervision, including the topics and cases discussed. Such documentation may be requested by licensing boards, insurance carriers or other professional entities.

A) There's no need to document clinical supervision.

It's both the supervisor's and the supervisee's responsibility to document that clinical supervision has taken place and what topics have been discussed.

B) Both the supervisor and the supervisee should document clinical supervision.

The supervisor and the supervisee should both keep careful documentation about clinical supervision.

C) The supervisor should carefully document the topics covered in supervision.

The supervisee should also document supervision.

D) The social worker receiving supervision can choose to take notes as desired.

It's important that both the supervisor and the supervisee document supervision.

59. A social worker receives a phone call from a client who's been meeting with the social worker for several months. The client is crying and tells the social worker that she was raped by a neighbor earlier in the day. What should the social worker do FIRST?

Medical attention following a sexual assault can help test for pregnancy or STDs, provide preventative medical care, and help gather evidence in the event the victim chooses to report the crime to the police.

A) The social worker should recommend the client come to the office for an immediate appointment.

The social worker should first recommend medical care.

B) The social worker should recommend the client contact the police.

Many people choose not to report a rape to the police. The social worker can talk to the victim about making a report, but the imperative first step is to seek medical treatment.

C) The social worker should make a mandated report to the police to report the crime.

Unless the victim is a child, it's up to the client to make a report or not.

D) The social worker should recommend the client seek immediate medical attention.

For a variety of medical and legal reasons, immediate medical treatment is the proper first step.

60. Which of the following is an example of an administrative supervisor's duty?

The NASW identifies three different type of social work supervisory positions: administrative, educational, and supportive. Administrative supervision focuses on how the agency's policies and organizational structure impact a social worker's performance.

A) Discussing how the agency's policies impact the supervisee's service to clients.

An administrative supervisor reviews how an agency's policies and the agency's organizational structure impact a social worker's job.

B) Making suggestions about a social worker's treatment interventions.

Discussing a social worker's treatment interventions is the role of an educational supervisor.

C) Discussing the supervisee's approach to treatment planning.

Discussing a social worker's approach to treatment planning is one of the roles of an educational supervisor.

D) The supervisor helps reduce job stress so the social worker can provide services more effectively.

Reducing a social worker's job stress is a supportive supervisor's duty.

61. An outpatient social worker meets with a man who has been diagnosed with schizophrenia. The man takes medication and states he finds it helpful. He continues to report strong beliefs in paranormal activity and attends weekly meetings with others who share his beliefs. How should the social worker proceed with this man's treatment?

Religion and spirituality, including a supportive church environment, can play a beneficial role in the lives of people with schizophrenia. On the other hand, clients with schizophrenia may risk ostracism by religious groups. A social worker should explore spiritual beliefs with clients with schizophrenia to discuss how their beliefs may or may not help relieve their symptoms, while making sure to respect the clients' rights to their beliefs.

A) The social worker should include discussions about the man's belief systems and how it may or may not relate to his symptoms.

Although the man may find comfort in spending time with people who share his beliefs, it's important for the social worker to explore how these beliefs may or may not be related to his schizophrenia.

B) The social worker should treat the schizophrenia without addressing the man's reports of paranormal activity.

Rather than ignore the man's spiritual beliefs, the social worker should explore how these beliefs may or may not be affecting his schizophrenia.

C) The social worker should consider the client's beliefs in paranormal activity as symptoms of his schizophrenia.

It's important for the social worker to respect this man's spiritual beliefs, since they may or may not be implicated in his schizophrenia.

D) The social worker should discourage the man from attending groups who believe in paranormal activity, since such beliefs can fuel his symptoms.

Since there's no evidence the group sessions are harmful, it would be disrespectful and inappropriate for the social worker to discourage the client from attending them.

62. A child in a Latino family is being picked on by peers. The child's teacher has reported the child exhibits some behavior problems. In a typical, traditional Latino family, the person MOST likely to address the problems with the school is:

Traditional Latino culture often relies heavily on the concept of machismo for men and marianismo for women. Ideal characteristics for men include pride, honor, courage, and leadership; for women, self-sacrifice and subordination.

A) The grandmother.

Grandmothers don't tend to make the decisions in most Latino families.

B) Both parents together.

Generally, it is the father who is head of the household in a Latino family and therefore the best choice to deal with this situation.

C) The father.

Since Latino men tend to be the head of household, it's likely the father would handle this issue.

D) The mother.

> *In traditional Latino families, women typically defer to their husbands to make important decisions, especially when dealing with children and authority figures.*

63. Taijin kyofusho and shenjing shuairuo are examples of:

Culture-specific syndromes don't neatly conform to Western categorization of mental illness, and are only found within certain ethnic populations. Examples include ataque de nervios, dhat syndrome, khyâl cap, kufungisisa, maladi moun, shenjing shuairuo, susto, and taijin kyofusho.

A) Japanese mental illnesses

> *Both are culture-specific syndromes, one Japanese, the other Chinese.*

B) Holistic medications

> *Taijin kyofusho and shenjing shuairuo are culture-bound syndromes, not types of medication.*

C) Culture-specific syndromes

> *Taijin kyofusho is a culturally distinctive phobia, found in Japan, that refers to an intense fear that one's body, its parts or its functions, displease, embarrass, or are offensive to other people. Shenjing shuairuo, which is found in primarily in China, , refers to physical or mental fatigue and excitability--something akin to a "nervous breakdown."*

D) Depressive syndromes

> *Taijin kyofusho involves an anxious shame about one's body, shenjing shuairuo is a mixed symptom episode.*

64. A social worker meets with a Russian immigrant who was referred by his primary care physician. The social worker asks the man whether or not there's a family history of mental illness. The man refuses to answer. How should the social worker proceed?

People from Russia tend to view mental illness as disgraceful and are not likely to be forthcoming about their family's history of mental illness. The social worker should respect the client's culture and not attempt to force an answer.

A) The social worker should stress the importance of obtaining information about the family's history of mental illness.

   Trying to force this client to answer the question would demonstrate a lack of respect for his culture.

B) Ask the man why he won't answer the question.

   The social worker should be aware of Russian sensitivities in this area, and not pry into his reasons for not answering.

C) Make note of the man's choice not to answer and move on to the next question.

   Since this client's refusal to answer is typical of Russian culture, the respectful approach is to honor his choice not to talk about his family's history of mental illness.

D) The social worker should ask the question in another way to make sure the client understands what information is being sought.

   Asking the question another way is not likely to be helpful and may make this client feel uncomfortable. If the social worker feels the client is truly struggling to understand questions, an interpreter is warranted.

65. Which of the following is true of culture-bound syndromes?

In DSM-5, "culture-bound syndromes" are reconceived as "cultural concepts of distress." In addition to being included in an appendix, they are incorporated throughout the manual.

A) Culture-bound syndromes have been incorporated throughout DSM-5.

   References to cultural concepts of distress appear throughout DSM-5 as well as in the appendix.

B) Attention to specific cultural presentation has been dropped in DSM-5.

   Cultural concepts of distress have been incorporated throughout DSM-5.

C) Culture-bound syndromes are no longer diagnosed because they're a function of people's culture and not their mental health.

   Culture-bound syndromes--now "cultural concepts in distress"--are a valuable part of understanding of clients' mental health.

D) Culture-bound syndromes can only be diagnosed by a physician, since they refer to physical health issues.

Culture-bound syndromes can refer to either physical or mental health issues.

66. A mother refers her six-year-old son to a social worker. During the initial intake, the mother, who is biracial, says her son is racist. She states that he regularly says things like "White people are better." She wants the social worker to address this issue with her son. How should the social worker respond?

Children learn stereotypes and racism from other people. It would be important to inquire further about where this child is learning these messages before determining what course of action to take.

A) Explain that racial stereotyping is part of normal identity development in children with biracial parents.

Although it's normal for children to have questions about race and skin color, they don't usually declare one race is superior to others unless they've heard it from adults.

B) Agree to educate the child about race and equality.

Until the social worker know where the child is learning racist messages, this approach is unlikely to be successful.

C) Inquire about where the child may be learning these attitudes.

The first step is to determine where the child is picking up racist messages. If it happens that the child is learning these attitudes from family members, a systemic intervention may be most effective.

D) Explain that the child is likely making racist comments to get attention.

There's no indication that the child is saying these things to provoke attention.

67. Accepting gifts from clients:

Gifts aren't directly addressed in the NASW Code of Ethics. Care should be taken to avoid creating a dual relationship and to maintain professional boundaries. Although it isn't usually appropriate to accept gifts from clients, in some cultures refusing a gift may be seen as offensive, especially when it comes to food. Social workers should be aware of a client's cultural norms and be willing to behave in a way that shows cultural sensitivity.

A) May be acceptable depending on the client's culture.

> *If refusing a gift is likely to offend the client, the social worker should consider accepting it.*

B) Is never acceptable.

> *There are circumstances in which accepting the gift is appropriate, especially when refusing a gift amounts to a cultural insult.*

C) Is always acceptable.

> *There are many times that accepting a gift is unethical, e.g., when a gift is extravagant or seems to come with strings attached.*

D) Is only acceptable if the client insists.

> *A client's insistence shouldn't be the determining factor. For example, if an elderly client insists on paying a social worker for helping to find a nursing home for her husband, it would be inappropriate to accept.*

68. A social worker meets with a five-year-old child and his parents. The parents are concerned about the child's oppositional behavior. Asking about the parents' cultural beliefs during the intake:

Since cultural issues may impact how parents expect a child to behave, how they perceive a child's role in the family and how they believe discipline should be handled, social workers should inquire about the parents' culture to learn about its possible influence on their parenting practices.

A) Would be inappropriate in front of the child, so the social worker should first ask the child to leave the room.

> *Asking the child to leave the room could send the message that the family's culture is shameful.*

B) Would only be appropriate if the social worker suspects their beliefs about parenting fall outside the social norm.

> *The social worker should ask the question regardless of whether or not the social worker thinks the parents' beliefs are unusual.*

C) Would be appropriate, because the parents' culture can influence their parenting practices.

It's important for social workers to inquire about the possible impact of people's culture on their parenting.

D) Would be inappropriate, because the family may assume the social worker is blaming the child's behavior on cultural issues.

If the social worker asks about the family's culture in a respectful and direct manner, such questions are not likely to offend.

69. A social worker meets with a family who moved to the United States from Mexico 10 years ago. The social worker asks questions such as, "In what language are the TV programs you watch?" and "Throughout your adult life, have most of your neighbors been Mexican Americans?" What is the MOST likely reason that the social worker is asking these questions?

Acculturation refers to how much a member of one culture group has adopted the beliefs of another group. A person's acculturation can impact how they feel about their environment. While some people prefer to preserve their original heritage, others prefer to adopt the behaviors of the dominant group.

A) The social worker is determining how much of a language barrier is likely present.

The social worker can determine language barriers by asking more direct questions about a family's understanding of the English language and by paying attention to their ability to answer questions appropriately. A family could continue to live by their cultural beliefs and still have a good command of English.

B) The social worker is trying to determine if the family is in the United States legally.

The social worker is not likely inquiring about the family's immigration status because the social worker would provide services irrelevant of their immigration status.

C) The social worker is trying to establish rapport with the family.

Asking questions about the family's acculturation is not likely to help the social worker to build rapport.

D) The social worker is trying to learn about the family's degree of acculturation.

Asking about the family's language and social relationships would likely tell the social worker the extent to which a family has adopted the beliefs and behaviors of the dominant culture.

70. A social worker meets with parents and a teenager who was born male but identifies as female. The teen wants to begin transitioning socially to a female by wearing female clothing and requesting being called "she." The parents want the teen to identify as male, because they'are greatly concerned about bullying and safety. How should the social worker proceed?

Social workers working with transgender teenagers and their families should provide support to both the teenager and the family, helping them evaluate the pros and cons of making a social transition to the other gender, and leaving the final decision to the teenager.

A) Since the parents disagree with the teenager, the social worker should discourage the social transition, which will most likely increase family conflict.

   Although it may increase conflict, the social worker shouldn't automatically discourage this teen from making the social change, which could have benefits as well.

B) The social worker should discourage the teen from making the social transition until adulthood.

   Many transgender teenagers make successful social transitions before adulthood.

C) **The social worker should help the teenager and the parents weigh the pros and cons of making the social transition.**

   Since the decision is ultimately the teenager's, the social worker's role is to educate the teenager and the family about the benefits and risks of making the transition.

D) The social worker should begin helping the teen with the social transition.

   The social worker should not simply begin to work with the teen on transitioning without first discussing the pros and cons of transitioning with the teen and family.

71. A hospital social worker meets with a family--a mother, father, 12-year-old boy and 8-year-old girl. The 12-year-old boy has been diagnosed with muscular dystrophy and his health has declined to the point that he requires the use of a wheelchair much of the time. The mother used to work as a nurse but became a stay-at-home parent when their son became ill. The father has recently stopped working due to a back injury. What is one of the MOST important issues the social worker should check in to see how the child's illness is affecting this family?

When one member of a family has a chronic illness, it impacts everyone in the family. The stress of caring for an ill family member can take a toll, and caregivers are sometimes hesitant to ask for help or unsure where to find help.

A) The social worker should determine if the parents are experiencing caregiver fatigue and see if they have enough support to help them care for their son.

> *Since the father has a back injury, he may not be able to provide physical support to the child, and the bulk of the responsibility may fall on the mother. Caregiver burnout can lead to mental health issues and relationship problems, so it's important for this social worker to learn how the parents are coping with the child's illness and see if this family needs any assistance.*

B) The social worker should see if the 8-year-old daughter is experiencing any behavioral issues due to her brother's illness.

> *Although it may be important to check in to see how the sibling is doing, it's more important to make sure that the boy's needs are being met first, and if caregiver fatigue is making it difficult to address other issues.*

C) The social worker should see if the child's school is meeting his educational needs and whether the family needs help advocating for their son.

> *Although the child's education is important, the priority is to make sure his needs are being met at home.*

D) The social worker should see if the 12-year-old child is experiencing any side effects from his medications.

> *If the child is experiencing any side effects of his medication, these issues should be addressed with the doctors and not the social worker.*

72. Which of the following is true about methylphenidate (Ritalin)?

Methylphenidate (Ritalin), a stimulant that helps decrease hyperactivity and improve impulse control, is commonly prescribed for ADHD.

A) Ritalin is a sedative that is commonly prescribed for ADHD.

> *Ritalin is a stimulant.*

B) Ritalin was banned from the marketplace as a result of black box warnings.

> *Ritalin continues to be prescribed for people of all ages with ADHD.*

C) Ritalin is a stimulant commonly prescribed for ADHD.

> *Ritalin is a stimulant that activates parts of the brain responsible for concentration and impulse control, and is often prescribed for ADHD.*

D) Ritalin is not safe for children under the age of 18.

Ritalin is prescribed for people of all ages with ADHD.

73. People who complete suicide usually:

People with substance-abuse disorders and mental illness--particularly depressive disorders--are at especially high risk for completing suicide.

A) Have some type of mental illness or substance-abuse problem.

More than 90 percent of people who complete suicide have a mental illness.

B) Do not have any sign of prior mental illness.

Most people who complete suicide have a mental illness.

C) Have borderline personality disorder.

Though most people who complete suicide have a mental illness, it's usually a depressive disorder or a substance abuse problem, not borderline personality disorder.

D) Under the age of 18.

White men over the age of 85 have the highest suicide rates.

74. A social worker meets with a nine-year-old child and her parents. The parents report the child is anxious, complains of a stomach ache in the mornings and tries to miss the bus to school. They say the anxiety has increased so for the past two weeks they have allowed her to stay home from school. What should the social worker recommend FIRST?

School refusal can stem from a variety of problems. Anxiety is a common reason kids stay home. However, keeping a child at home is likely to worsen the child's anxiety, not relieve it. When parents allow children to stay home from school, it can create more problems for the child--as well as legal problems for the parents.

A) The social worker should recommend the parents find a tutor to help the child stay caught up on her school work.

Although a tutor can help ensure the child stays caught up with her academics, it will not solve her problems with anxiety.

B) **The social worker should recommend the child return to school as soon as possible.**

Not sending the child to school is illegal. Although these parents are well-intentioned in their attempts to reduce their daughter's anxiety, they are likely going to make her anxiety worse in the long-term if they do not make her attend school.

C) The social worker should advocate for the child with the school to see how the child's needs can be met.

There is no indication that the school is not meeting the child's needs.

D) The social worker should recommend that the child continue to stay home until she has made enough progress in treatment to return to school.

The longer the child avoids school the more difficult it could be for her to return. The social worker will likely be most successful in treating the child's anxiety with exposure to school, not continued avoidance.

75. A 50-year-old man with cirrhosis of the liver was referred to a social worker by his primary care physician. The man drinks up to four cans of beer per day. He states he doesn't think alcohol is a problem, and denies his liver is as bad as his doctor says. The social worker assigns the man homework to help him cut down on his alcohol consumption, but the man never completes his homework and continues to drink at the same rate. What is MOST likely happening?

It's important for social workers to identify a client's stage of change. According to the Transtheoretical Model, clients who are precontemplative don't acknowledge a problem and have no desire to change. When clients are precontemplative, the best approach is to help them identify the pros and cons of their current behavior without trying to convince them that they need to change.

A) The social worker hasn't helped the man gain enough social support to help him quit drinking.

Social support isn't likely to be helpful until the man acknowledges he has a problem and is ready to change.

B) The man likely doesn't understand his homework assignments and his refusal to participate is the result of his confusion.

There's no evidence that this man doesn't understand the homework assignments.

C) The man is most likely precontemplative and isn't ready to commit to making any changes.

> *Since the man doesn't acknowledge the accuracy of the diagnosis, and denies he has any problem with alcohol, he's precontemplative--resistant not only to making changes but also to the homework the social worker is prematurely assigning. .*

D) The man is most likely contemplative about his drinking but not yet ready to commit to change.

> *There's no indication that the man is thinking about whether he has a problem.*

76. Treating combat veterans for PTSD can be complicated, owing to difficulties encountered during exposure therapy. A successful treatment modality for many soldiers has included:

Virtual reality therapy allows clinicians to simulate the combat environment and expose soldiers to lifelike scenarios, thereby helping reduce their anxiety and symptoms of PTSD.

A) Psychoanalytic therapy.

> *There's conflicting research about the benefits of psychoanalysis and PTSD. For soldiers who develop symptoms due to combat experience, exploring their childhood or their unconscious desires hasn't proven helpful.*

B) Virtual reality therapy.

> *Virtual reality therapy, which seems to reduce the stigma surrounding treatment, has been shown to be effective in reducing symptoms of PTSD for combat soldiers.*

C) Sand tray therapy.

> *Sand tray therapy is most commonly used with children, since they're less likely to be able to verbalize their experiences.*

D) Hypnotherapy.

> *There is conflicting research about whether or not hypnotherapy is helpful for symptoms of PTSD.*

77. Six students at the same rural high school have died by suicide over the past two years. This high rate of suicide is MOST likely to:

High suicide rates in communities can be a risk factor for further suicides, sometimes to epidemic proportions, if suicide becomes normalized as a way to solve problems.

A) Be a risk factor that can lead to increased suicides by other people in the community.

A high number of suicides in a community can trigger future suicides.

B) Not influence the suicide rate in the community one way or the other.

A high rate of suicide is likely to cause further suicides and suicide attempts in the community.

C) Only affect the suicide rate if the previous suicides were interrelated.

Whether or not the previous suicides were connected, a high rate of suicide is likely to increase the overall risk for the community.

D) Be a protective factor leading to decreased suicide in the community.

A high rate of suicide is likely to increase the rate of future suicides.

78. Being raised by a single mother places children MOST at risk for:

Children who are raised by single mothers are most at risk for living in poverty and developing physical health issues. Even if children raised by single mothers don't live below the poverty line, they tend to have more health issues than their peers.

A) Low IQ and academic problems.

Being raised by a single mother is not an indicator of low IQ and does not necessarily place children at higher risk for developing academic problems.

B) ADHD and bipolar disorder.

A few studies indicate children with single parents are diagnosed with ADHD more often, but there's no evidence they're more likely to have bipolar disorder.

C) Developmental delays and peer problems.

Except in cases of neglect, children raised by single mothers are not at more risk for developmental problems, and there's no evidence they're more likely to have peer problems; some studies indicate children raised by single parents form more friendships than other children.

D) Poverty and physical health problems.

Children raised by single mothers are more at risk for poverty and health problems.

79. Which of the following underlying theories are a basis for cognitive-behavioral therapy?

Cognitive behavioral therapy is based on a combination of behavioral theory, cognitive theory, and social learning theory. CBT recognizes that people learn behavior when it's modeled for them by others, and that their thoughts and expectations can play a major role in determining behavior. The therapy helps people change maladaptive behavior and identify and replace cognitive distortions.

A) Family systems theory.

> *Family systems theory is based on the assumption that people cannot be understood as separate individuals but only as part of their family; cognitive-behavior therapy focuses on people's thoughts and behaviors rather than their family relationships.*

B) Psychodynamic theory.

> *Psychodynamic psychotherapy addresses unconscious and internal processes that motivate behavior; cognitive-behavior therapy is based on conscious thoughts.*

C) Conflict theory.

> *Conflict theory is based on the idea that groups and individuals try to advance their own interests over the interests of others, who may feel oppressed as a result; it's not a central part of cognitive-behavior therapy.*

D) Social learning theory.

> *Social learning theory states that people learn behavior by watching others. CBT recognizes that people can learn behavior when it is modeled for them by others. Also, a person's thoughts influences a person's behavior so a person's expectations can play a major role in determining behavior.*

80. Which of the following is considered a protective factor for suicide?

Knowing the risk factors for suicide can help a social worker determine a client's suicide risk, and being aware of the protective factors can help reduce that risk.

A) Being unmarried.

> *Being unmarried increases a person's risk for suicide.*

B) Being male.

> *Males have an increased risk for suicide.*

C) Being over the age of 70.

People over the age of 70 have an increased risk for suicide.

D) Having children in the home.

Having children in the home, or caring for children, can reduce a person's risk for suicide.

81. Which of these is true about the short-term effects of marijuana?

Marijuana can have a variety of short-term effects, including a distorted sense of time, vision and hearing distortions, sleepiness, lack of coordination, reddening of the eyes, muscle relaxation, and increased heart rate.

A) Increased energy and confidence, involuntary teeth-clenching, and blurred vision.

These symptoms are more indicative of the short-term effects of ecstasy.

B) Tremors, vertigo, muscle twitches, paranoia, and anxiety.

These symptoms are more indicative of the short-term effects of cocaine.

C) Relaxed muscles, increased heart rate, and a distorted sense of time.

Relaxed muscles, increased heart rate and a distorted sense of time are common short-term effects of marijuana use.

D) Increased respiration, increased physical activity, and irregular heartbeat.

These symptoms are more indicative of the short-term effects of methamphetamine.

82. A social worker begins meeting with a woman who states her husband has abused her verbally for the past 15 years, and physically for the last two. This is the first time she has reached out for help. According to a family systems perspective, what is MOST likely to happen initially if this woman tries to become more assertive?

According to family systems theory, families try to maintain a constant balance, or homeostasis. When one family member makes a change, the others make corresponding changes to ensure the dynamics remain fundamentally the same.

A) The husband will become more aggressive in an attempt to maintain homeostasis.

If this client becomes more assertive, it's likely her husband will increase his aggression to make sure she doesn't gain more power and control.

B) A second order change is likely to take place.

A second order change refers to a later transformation within the system, not an initial one.

C) The husband won't change his behavior.

If the wife changes her behavior, it's likely the husband will alter his in order to maintain the basic family dynamic.

D) The husband will become less aggressive in an attempt to give his wife more freedom.

According to family systems theory, it's unlikely this man would welcome a change in the family dynamic.

83. A mother meets with a social worker because her ten-year-old son has been exhibiting unusual, sexualized behavior. The mother is concerned that he may have been sexually abused. What might the social worker tell the mother regarding the most common characteristics of perpetrators?

Statistically, most sexual perpetrators are adult males who are familiar with their victim. Many of them have a history of sexual abuse, mental illness, and alcohol or drug problems.

A) Perpetrators are often females in a position of authority, such as teaching.

It is usually male perpetrators who sexually abuse both male and female children.

B) The majority of perpetrators are family members who are under the age of 18.

Most perpetrators are adults.

C) Most perpetrators are adult males who are known and trusted by the child.

Most perpetrators are adult males who are familiar with the child, with whom they have developed a trusting relationship.

D) Most perpetrators are males who meet their victims over the Internet.

Most perpetrators are family members or neighbors.

84. A social worker meets with a recently widowed man. The man says his dog seems very sad and lonely since the wife's death. What defense mechanism is the man MOST likely exhibiting?

Defense mechanisms are ways people protect themselves against painful feelings. When people use projection, they tend to attribute their thoughts and feelings to others.

A) Repression

Repression refers to blocking unacceptable thoughts and feelings from consciousness.

B) Projection

In attributing to his dog what he is most likely feeling himself, this man is exhibiting projection.

C) Denial

A person using denial refuses to acknowledge that a painful event or feeling ever existed.

D) Compartmentalization

Compartmentalization refers to the process of isolating two or more conflicting values or beliefs from each other. For example, people may value honesty in their home life but lie to get ahead at work.

85. A mother meets with a social worker because she is worried about her 16-year-old son's substance abuse. She reports catching him smoking marijuana several times. He says pot is "not a big deal" and is not interested in seeking help. What is the BEST suggestion the social worker can make to ensure the mother does not enable her son?

When parents enable their children to use drugs, they make it easier for their teens to have a substance abuse problem. Giving teens an allowance when they have a substance abuse problem can help them purchase more drugs.

A) The social worker should advise the mother to stop spending time with her son as punishment for his drug use.

The social worker should not advise this mother to punish her teen by not spending time with him. This could exacerbate the substance use, not lessen it.

B) The social worker should advise the mother to stop giving her son an allowance, since he might use the money to buy drugs.

It is appropriate for the social worker to recommend that his mother not give her son money as he is likely using it to buy marijuana.

C) The social worker should advise the mother to take her son to see a substance abuse counselor whether he wants to or not.

Counseling might be helpful, but if the teen is refusing treatment, the mother would likely have little success getting him to attend or participate.

D) The social worker should advise the mother to kick her son out of the house immediately until he has quit using drugs.

Since the client's son is a minor, the social worker should not advise this woman to kick her son out of the house.

86. Personality disorders are MOST likely caused by:

Research indicates that a combination of genetic and environmental factors can lead to personality disorders, including childhood trauma, verbal abuse and peer relationships. Children with high reactivity and sensitivity are also at risk for personality disorders.

A) Childhood trauma.

Various genetic and environmental factors contribute to the development of personality disorders.

B) A combination of factors, including genetics, childhood trauma, and peer relationships.

Personality disorders most likely result from a variety of genetic and environmental factors.

C) Genetics.

Environmental factors are also likely to contribute to personality disorder development.

D) Peer relationships.

Other environmental factors, as well as genetics, can contribute to the development of a personality disorder.

87. Reactive attachment disorder is primarily caused by:

Reactive attachment disorder causes children to struggle to manage their own emotions as well as to connect with caregivers. Common reasons babies develop attachment problems include not being comforted when crying, being ignored for hours on end, being separated from caregivers, or having emotionally unavailable parents.

A) Genetics.

Reactive attachment disorder is not primarily genetic.

B) A child's behavior problem that causes caregiver stress.

Although children with attachment disorders have behavior problems, it's more likely their behavior problems resulted from the attachment disorder rather than their behavior disrupted the relationship with the caregiver.

C) Neglect, a parent's emotional unavailability or disruption in caregivers.

When a baby's needs are neglected, or a parent doesn't connect emotionally, reactive attachment disorder can develop. A child's separation from caregivers, as a result of being placed in foster care or hospitalization, can also lead to attachment problems.

D) Sexual abuse or physical abuse.

Although abuse can certainly result in attachment problems, neglect is more commonly the cause. Children who are abused sometimes still get their needs met, and can receive a degree of love and affection.

88. A social worker conducts an assessment on a seven-year-old boy. The boy's parents state that he doesn't listen, he's having trouble in school, and his out-of-control behavior is causing marital distress for his parents and academic problems for his 12-year-old sister. From a family systems perspective, what is MOST likely happening?

Family therapy views the family as a dynamic whole, in which one family member can sometimes be scapegoated for everyone else's issues--in this case, the parents' marriage and the sister's academic problems.

A) The family hierarchy is such that the boy has equal power with his parents.

There's no evidence that this child has power equal to his parents' in the family system.

B) The boy's mental illness is causing the parents' marital distress.

From a family systems perspective, the parents' marital distress might well be the source of the boy's misbehavior, not the other way around.

C) The boy is the scapegoat for the family's problems.

Since this family identifies the boy's behavior as the source of all their problems, it's most likely they're scapegoating him.

D) The older sister likely has more problems than her parents realize.

There's no indication that the older sister has problems other than her school issues.

89. A social worker has been meeting with an elderly man in a nursing home. The man states he just learned his teenage grandson was severely beaten by another teenager. The man says he would like to hunt down the other teenager and shoot him. How should the social worker respond FIRST?

A social worker should explore a person's threats to see if they are credible or not. Although this man is in a nursing home, and most likely does not have access to weapons--or the potential victim--it's still important to assess the risk level before determining a course of action.

A) The social worker should validate the man's feelings of anger and question whether or not he has any further intent.

Although this man probably lacks the means and opportunity to carry out his threat, the social worker should further question his intent, after first validating his feelings of anger.

B) The social worker should contact the police so the victim can be notified that a threat was made against his life.

The social worker should not contact the police until a further assessment has been made to determine if there is a credible threat.

C) The social worker should notify the nursing home staff of the man's threats so they can keep him under high alert.

Before alerting the nursing home staff, the social worker should first talk to the man about his intentions to carry out the threat.

D) The social worker should remind the man that making such threats can lead to serious consequences.

Lecturing the man about making threats may cause him to feel he's being treated like a child. The priority is to assess the risk level by asking further questions.

90. A school social worker meets with a 13-year-old girl. The girl states that she keeps getting into trouble because her peers "dare" her to do things or because she follows the crowd. She regrets many of her decisions and states she wants to "get things back in order." What intervention is likely to be the MOST helpful?

Teaching children how to say "no" and stand up for themselves can be one of the best ways for them to resist peer pressure. The more confident children become about their ability to say "no," the more likely they are to resist negative pressures.

A) Teaching her assertiveness skills.

> *Teaching this child assertiveness skills is likely to help her refuse to participate in activities which make her uncomfortable.*

B) Reviewing her earliest experiences of being peer-pressured.

> *Reviewing her history isn't likely to help her resist future instances of peer pressure.*

C) Exploring her feelings of guilt.

> *Simply exploring her feelings of guilt isn't likely to help her resist peer pressure the next time she's exposed to it.*

D) Conducting a group intervention with her friends.

> *Although a group intervention may be helpful in the short-term, it isn't likely to have lasting effect. A better approach is to help this child learn to resist peer pressure in general, by teaching her assertiveness skills.*

91. A social worker focusing on what the client wants his future life to be like is using which therapeutic approach?

Solution focused therapy emphasizes a person's goals rather than their symptoms or presenting problems.

A) Solution focused

> *Solution focused therapy directs a person's attention to the future and how to change in order to reach their goals.*

B) Existential

> *Existential therapy focuses on the whole person, with an emphasis on choice and human limitation.*

C) Object Relations

> *Object relations therapy focuses on how a person is shaped by others in the environment.*

D) Psychoanalytic

> *Psychoanalytic therapy focuses on how the unconscious mind influences a person's thoughts and behaviors.*

92. One of the most effective interventions for people with antisocial personality disorder is:

Antisocial personality disorder can be very difficult to treat. Direct confrontation can be effective, but not always when a professional is confronting the antisocial behaviors. Peer group interventions can sometimes be more helpful in motivating a person to change.

A) Cognitive behavioral therapy, focusing on irrational thinking.

> *Cognitive behavioral therapy isn't usually effective with antisocial personality disorder.*

B) The use of peer communities to confront behavior and promote change.

> *Allowing peers to directly confront a person's antisocial behaviors can be the most effective tool in creating change.*

C) Family therapy with an emphasis on addressing past attachment issues.

> *Family therapy isn't usually effective with people with antisocial personality disorder.*

D) A humanistic approach that offers unconditional positive regard.

> *A humanistic approach isn't likely to be effective for a person with antisocial personality disorder.*

93. An oncology social worker is working with a family in which the teenage daughter has been diagnosed with a rare but terminal form of cancer. The girl and her parents are hopeful for a miracle, despite hearing from the oncologist that the cancer is terminal. Given the family's reaction, how should the social worker proceed?

When people are given a terminal diagnosis, maintaining hope and optimism can reduce their depression and anxiety and lead to better outcomes.

A) The social worker should meet separately with the teenager to ensure she understands the cancer is terminal.

> *It's more helpful to encourage the family to remain hopeful, rather than reminding the teenager that her cancer is terminal.*

B) The social worker should gently remind the girl and her family that the cancer is terminal.

> *The fact that this family are praying for a miracle indicates they already understand the cancer is terminal.*

C) The social worker should help the family focus on their optimism.

> *Since there are cases in which people survive after a terminal diagnosis, it's for the social worker to help the family remain optimistic.*

D) The social worker should help the family move through the other stages of grief, since they're most likely in denial.

> *Since this family reports they're praying for a miracle, they understand the illness has a poor prognosis and therefore aren't in denial.*

94. Habit reversal is a technique that has shown to be effective in treating:

Habit reversal has been shown to be effective in treating hair pulling, nail biting, skin picking, and tics. In this behavioral intervention, people become aware of their behavior and learn to replace or prevent it.

A) Trichotillomania

> *Trichotillomania (hair pulling disorder) has shown to be effectively treated with habit reversal.*

B) Attention deficit hyperactivity disorder

> *Habit reversal is not commonly used in cases of ADHD, which is more often treated through parental training and educating clients about coping skills.*

C) Obsessive-compulsive disorder

> *Obsessive-compulsive disorder is usually treated with exposure therapy.*

D) Specific phobias

> *Specific phobias are most commonly treated with exposure therapy.*

95. A social worker meets with a 70-year-old man who meets the criteria for major depression. The man lives alone and has been experiencing increased physical health problems. During the initial interview, the MOST important thing is for the social worker to:

Older people are at increased risk for suicide. Since this man has major depression, it's imperative that the social worker assess his risk during the first interview.

A) Gather personal and family history.

Obtaining history is less important than determining the client's risk for suicide.

B) Determine if the client needs help doing activities around his home.

Although the client might need help with activities of daily living, it's more important to first assess his risk for suicide.

C) Assess the client's risk for suicide.

Since this client might be in immediate danger, it's important to assess his risk for suicide during the initial interview.

D) Determine the client's strengths.

Although assessing strengths is important, determining if the client is at risk for suicide takes priority.

96. A social worker meets with the family of a 23-year-old man who has been hospitalized for bizarre behaviors at work, and subsequently diagnosed with schizophrenia. What type of intervention is likely going to be MOST helpful for the family at this time?

When a person is diagnosed with schizophrenia, it's important for the family to be educated about the diagnosis. People with schizophrenia often benefit greatly from having supportive family members who are able to recognize changes in symptoms and functioning.

A) The social worker should conduct family therapy that includes the client, so the family can process what led to his admission.

The man is likely to find family therapy too difficult at this point.

B) The social worker should educate the family about the man's diagnosis and what they might expect in the future.

Educating the family and answering any questions they might have about his prognosis is likely to be most beneficial to them and the client.

C) The social worker should discuss group home options with the family, since the man will likely need ongoing support.

There's no indication that this man will require residential care at this point. Many people with schizophrenia are able to live independently.

D) The social worker should give the family information about obtaining guardianship of the man.

> *There's no evidence this man can't be his own guardian. Many people with schizophrenia are able to serve as their own guardians.*

97. The purpose of a psychoeducational substance-abuse group is MOST likely to:

A psychoeducational group provides information to its members about a particular issue, such as substance abuse, so that they can decide whether they want to make changes in their lives.

A) Help members identify and discuss how their early life experiences contribute to their substance abuse.

> *A psychodynamic approach connecting childhood issues to substance abuse is more indicative of interpersonal process group therapy.*

B) Help precontemplative or contemplative people develop a need to seek help by educating them about their disorder and the recovery options.

> *A psychoeducational group for substance abusers can help them decide if they want to make changes, and works best for people who are precontemplative or contemplative.*

C) Help members identify and change maladaptive thoughts and behaviors in order to maintain sobriety.

> *Identifying maladaptive thoughts and behaviors is more indicative of a cognitive behavioral therapy group.*

D) Help people maintain sobriety and gain self-esteem by discussing their daily struggles with other members of the group.

> *Sharing problems is more indicative of a support group, such as AA.*

98. A man seeks help from a social worker after the death of his wife from a brief illness. The man states he feels intense sadness and asks how long he should expect the grief to last. How should the social worker respond?

Grief is an individual process depending on many factors, including how much work people do to address their grief. There's no time frame.

A) Tell him that it takes about one year to recover from the loss of a spouse.

Since there's no predictable time frame for grief, it's important for this man to work on healing rather than wait for a specific amount of time to pass.

B) Tell him that intense grief usually lasts about six months.

Giving the man a time frame may encourage him to ignore any grief work, possibly leading to disappointment when the six months are up.

C) Explain that grief is different for everyone and there's no predictable time frame.

Since everyone grieves differently, it's appropriate to help the man find the best way to heal, rather than focus on a time frame.

D) Explain that most widowers remarry in about three years.

Citing a time frame for remarriage isn't likely to help the man, who needs to focus first on healing.

99. A social worker meets with a man who has a long history of severe alcohol abuse. The man states he has significantly cut back on his drinking over the past few years, but still drinks one or two beers daily. He's been with his girlfriend for over a year, and she's started attending AA with him. He states he's pleased about her show of support. Involving his girlfriend in treatment with the social worker:

Involving significant others in the treatment process can often be very helpful, especially in the case of substance abuse. Clients who are contemplative about making change are more likely to commit to change when a significant other becomes involved in the process.

A) Would likely threaten the social worker's therapeutic alliance with the client.

If the social worker makes sure the client feels comfortable about his girlfriend's attending treatment, her participation isn't likely to have a negative impact on the therapeutic alliance.

B) Is likely to increase the client's commitment to change and could be helpful to his treatment.

Involving the client's girlfriend can help increase his motivation to change.

C) Would likely only be helpful if his girlfriend has successfully recovered from her own substance-abuse issues in the past.

The client's girlfriend can be supportive, and her participation in treatment helpful, even without a personal history of substance abuse.

D) Would be inappropriate, because the client may feel the social worker and his girlfriend are ganging up on him.

If the social worker is careful not to align with the client's girlfriend, involving her in the treatment can be effective.

100. A social worker meets with a blended family that consists of a mother and biological teenage son, her husband and his biological teenage son, and a six-year-old child the couple had together. The social worker asks a family to create a "family sculpture." The purpose of family sculpting is MOST likely to:

Family sculpting is a technique that many family therapists use to identify relationships and communication patterns among family members. In this approach, family members are asked to stand in positions that represent the family. The proximity between family members and their body language provide information about their relationships.

A) Establish goals and create behavioral changes.

Family sculpting does not identify goals or behavioral changes.

B) Help the family resolve conflict without talking about it.

Family sculpting is an assessment tool and a way to begin talking about change, not a nonverbal intervention.

C) Look for solutions to the issues surrounding a blended family.

Family sculpting identifies the problems and not necessarily the solutions.

D) Identify each person's role in the family and their relational patterns.

Family sculpting can reveal each individual's personality, role within the family, and relationship to other family members.

101. Asking a client to recount traumatic memories over and over again:

Exposure therapy for trauma is a common cognitive behavioral approach, involving discussing traumatic memories to desensitize the client to the memories, in conjunction with relaxation techniques.

A) Is likely to retraumatize a client and should never be done.

If clients have sufficient coping skills, asking them to repeatedly discuss traumatic memories can help desensitize them to the memories.

B) Desensitizes a client when done in conjunction with relaxation training.

With the help of relaxation techniques, such as guided imagery, and repeated discussion of the trauma, clients can become desensitized to traumatic memories.

C) Should never be in done in outpatient settings because it can lead to increased suicide risk.

So long as clients have the coping skills to deal with the traumatic memories, exposure therapy can be conducted in outpatient settings.

D) Should only be done under hypnosis.

Exposure therapy for trauma doesn't need to be done under hypnosis.

102. A social worker at a long-term care facility is MOST likely to perform which of the following duties?

A social worker in a long-term care facility will likely have many different duties, including promoting interaction between the community and the residents, and linking residents with health resources in the area.

A) Inviting a local girl scout troop to sing to the residents and arranging for a podiatrist to visit patients at the facility.

It's likely that the social worker's duties would include fostering this sort of community participation and linking residents with health care services.

B) Documenting residents' medication and researching ways for the establishment to save money.

Documenting medication is more likely a job for the nursing staff, and though a social worker may be involved in grant writing, a social worker's primary duties in a medical facility are not likely to include cost-saving efforts.

C) Interviewing nurses applying for direct care positions and educating them about patients' needs.

Although a social worker may have some responsibility in educating nurses about the social or mental health needs of patients, it's not likely to be a principal role, and neither is interviewing nurses.

D) Establishing policies to reduce safety risks for residents unable to ambulate, and developing emergency preparedness plans.

Instituting safety policies for residents unable to walk is more likely a job for an occupational therapist or the nursing staff; emergency preparedness plans are usually done in conjunction with staff members who provide direct care.

103. A couple has been meeting with a social worker for three weeks. They report wanting to work on their marriage. Despite the social worker's attempts to set rules, they argue constantly over small details. The social worker responds by saying, "You two are really good at arguing." The social workers response is an example of:

A paradoxical intervention is sometimes considered a form of reverse psychology. Instead of telling clients not to do something, it requires the social worker to commend the client or ask for something in an attempt to achieve the opposite result. Paradoxical interventions should only be used with caution and when they won't cause harm.

A) Functional family therapy.

Functional family therapy is an intensive treatment that helps adolescents who are at risk of being removed from the home due to their behavior.

B) Unethical behavior.

A paradoxical intervention is unethical if it could cause harm to a client. For example, telling a client who tends to skip medication doses to not take his medication for a week would be unethical. This social worker does not recommend anything that would be unethical to this couple.

C) Solution focused therapy.

Solution focused therapy would help the couple consider how they would be acting different if they were getting along well and help identify ways to exhibit those behaviors.

D) A paradoxical intervention.

The social worker's remark about the couple's behavior is a paradoxical intervention. Instead of asking them to stop, their skill at arguing is highlighted.

104. A social worker meets with a blended family comprised of a mother and her 10-year-old son from a previous marriage, her second husband, and his 14-year-old son. Whenever the social worker asks the man a question, the woman tries to speak for her husband. The social worker changes seats and sits between the woman and the man. What intervention is the social worker likely using?

Boundary marking is a structural family therapy technique in which the social worker addresses boundary issues, diffusing inappropriate boundaries and reinforcing healthy ones.

A) Joining, a part of family therapy

Joining refers to establishing rapport with the family--for example, by using the same type of language the family uses.

B) Exposure therapy, a part of behavioral therapy

Exposure therapy refers to slowly exposing someone to an anxiety-provoking situation.

C) Boundary marking, a part of structural family therapy

By sitting between the husband and wife, helping him find his voice and reducing his wife's attempts to speak for him, the social worker is employing the boundary marking technique, an aspect of structural family therapy.

D) Shaping, part of behavior modification

Shaping refers to slowly changing a behavior with the use of rewards and punishments.

105. A man tells a social worker that he cheated on his wife. He states it only happened once, and his wife is not aware of the incident. He asks the social worker for his professional opinion about whether or not he should tell his wife about the infidelity. How should the social worker respond?

Social workers should be aware of how their own values may influence their practice, and allow clients to arrive at their own decisions.

A) The social worker should advise the man based on the social worker's own values.

Social workers should not impose their personal values on clients.

B) The social worker should recommend that the man begin couples therapy with his wife to address underlying marital issues.

There's no evidence that couples therapy is necessary at this time or that there are underlying issues that would require couples therapy.

C) **The social worker should help the man weigh the pros and cons of telling or not telling his wife.**

Rather than give an opinion about disclosing the infidelity, the social worker should help the man arrive at his own decision.

D) The social worker should advise the man to tell his wife, since keeping secrets will be harmful to his marriage.

The social worker should not assume that disclosing the infidelity will harm the marriage, but should encourage the man to consider the consequences either way.

106. A social worker meets with a 25-year-old woman who has recently been diagnosed with bipolar I. The woman describes having manic episodes that cause her to drive recklessly and engage in promiscuous sex. She states she has also had depressive episodes during which she was unable to get out of bed, and lost her job as a result. She's been placed on a mood stabilizer and says her mood now seems to be consistent. What intervention is likely to be MOST helpful to this client?

People with bipolar disorder experience both manic episodes and depressive episodes. Since mood stabilizers don't usually prevent all further episodes, it's important to teach people with bipolar how to recognize early warning signs of mood changes and triggers, so they can stabilize their moods over the long-term.

A) Psychoanalytic therapy to help her address past issues that are likely contributing to her mood.

Exploring clients' childhood issues isn't likely to help address their bipolar disorder.

B) Assertiveness training and advocacy to help her get her job back now that she's stabilized.

If this client didn't perform her job duties, she's more likely to benefit from looking for a new job.

C) **Teaching self-monitoring skills so she can recognize warning signs of mood changes and triggers.**

By teaching people with bipolar disorder how to recognize early warning signs of mood changes and triggers, a social worker can help them prevent manic or depressive episodes, as well as avoid situations that trigger mood changes.

D) The empty-chair technique in gestalt therapy, where she can learn to talk to her body about her symptoms.

Empty chair work isn't likely to help the client with her mood swings.

107. A social worker meets with a 25-year-old man who has Asperger's syndrome. He's fairly successful at his job as a biologist, but spends much of his time socially isolated, and feels depressed. The man says he's tried online dating, but after one or two dates, women usually tell him they just want to be friends. What sort of treatment is this man MOST likely to benefit from?

Adults with autism spectrum disorder (ASD) often lack understanding of social cues, including facial expressions. They may center their conversation on topics that interest them, and as a result may appear self-centered. With training in social skills, people with ASD can achieve successful relationships.

A) Supportive counseling that gives him a chance to talk about his feelings.

   Talking about his feelings can be helpful but is unlikely to improve his understanding of social cues.

B) Exposure therapy to reduce his anxiety about social situations.

   Since there's no evidence of social anxiety, this client's isolation is most likely caused by a lack of social skills, a common feature of ASD.

C) Social skills training to help reduce his isolation.

   Since the women he meets don't want to continue dating him, it's likely this client lacks social skills, and can benefit from training in this area.

D) Medication to reduce his depression.

   Although medication may relieve his depression, it isn't likely to reduce his social isolation.

108. A woman tells a social worker she doesn't bother to apply for jobs anymore because she won't get hired anyway. The social worker tells her to practice telling herself, "If I complete at least two job applications every day, it will increase the likelihood I'll find work." What technique is the social worker MOST likely using?

Cognitive restructuring--an aspect of cognitive therapy--involves replacing overly negative thoughts with more realistic thoughts. It can help people with a variety of conditions, including anxiety and depression.

A) Cognitive restructuring

   The social worker is recommending this woman change her negative thoughts to more realistic thoughts--an example of cognitive restructuring.

B) Mindfulness

Mindfulness entails focusing on what is happening in the moment.

C) Behavior therapy

The social worker is recommending that this woman change how she thinks, which represents a focus on cognition, not behavior.

D) Advocacy

The social worker recommending the woman change her thought patterns, not advocating she be hired.

109. A clinical social worker in an outpatient behavioral health center meets with a 30-year-old woman who reports a lot of anxiety and stress. She receives a monthly disability check but has difficulty managing her finances, which she says are the main source of her stress. The social worker detects the woman has some cognitive limitations and may be taken advantage of financially by others. What should the social worker do FIRST?

People with cognitive limitations are sometimes vulnerable to financial exploitation. In order to determine whether this woman is capable of managing her own finances, the social worker should refer her for a neuropsychological evaluation.

A) Recommend the woman take budgeting and finance classes through the local community center.

If this woman has cognitive limitations, the classes may only cause frustration and a feeling of incompetence. Instead, an evaluation should be conducted to determine if she's able to manage her finances.

B) Establish a monthly budget with the woman and assist her in following it.

Establishing a budget isn't the role of a clinical social worker. The proper course is to obtain a neuropsychological evaluation to determine if she can manage her finances on her own.

C) Explain to the woman that she needs a payee who can manage her money for her.

This social worker isn't yet certain whether or not this woman is able to manage her money, so it would be premature to recommend that this woman obtain a payee.

D) Refer this woman for a neuropsychological evaluation to see if she's able to manage her finances on her own.

Since there's doubt about the woman's cognitive abilities, it's appropriate to obtain an evaluation to determine if she can manage her money by herself.

110. A woman meets with a social worker because her four-year-old son has some behavioral issues, including constant whining. The social worker asks the woman how she responds to her son's whining. The woman says she tells him to stop but he doesn't listen. If the social worker is a firm believer in behavior modification, what is the MOST likely suggestion the social worker would make?

Behavior modification uses rewards to reinforce positive behaviors and punishments to discourage negative behaviors. Attention is considered a strong reinforcement, and ignoring is a punishment meant to extinguish a behavior.

A) The social worker would recommend the mother redirect the child's attention.

   Behavior modification uses direct rewards and punishments rather than redirection.

B) The social worker would recommend the mother validate the child's feelings.

   Behavior modification doesn't attempt to identify or validate the feelings underlying a negative behavior.

C) The social worker would recommend the mother ignore the child's whining.

   According to behavior modification, ignoring a negative behavior is likely to discourage the child from repeating the behavior.

D) The social worker would recommend the mother help the child identify his feelings.

   Behavior modification doesn't attempt to identify the underlying feelings.

111. A social worker has been meeting with a depressed woman for several months. The social worker encourages the woman to keep a journal. Each session they talk about her feelings, in order to help the woman gain a better understanding of herself. What intervention is the social worker MOST likely using?

In the humanistic approach, social workers help clients improve their self-concept and encourage feelings of self-worth, so they can work through their problems and recognize their full potential.

A) Psychoanalysis

Psychoanalysis explores a person's childhood and their unconscious drives and motives.

B) A humanistic approach

With journaling and talking about feelings front-and-center, the intervention is most likely a humanistic approach.

C) Cognitive behavioral therapy

CBT involves helping people change irrational thoughts and behaviors, with less emphasis on talking about feelings.

D) Solution-focused therapy

Solution- focused therapy is a short-term practice aimed at making concrete changes.

112. Which of the following usually begin during childhood or adolescence and are categorized as a neurodevelopmental disorder in DSM-5?

Tic disorders are usually diagnosed early in life. They are listed in the DSM-5 under neurodevelopmental disorders.

A) Anxiety disorders

Anxiety disorders can develop at any point in the life cycle and are not currently considered neurodevelopmental.

B) Mood disorders

Mood disorders can be diagnosed at any age. They are not categorized as neurodevelopmental in DSM-5.

C) Psychotic disorders

Psychotic disorders are listed under "Schizophrenia Spectrum and Other Disorders" in DSM-5 and can be diagnosed at any point in the life cycle.

D) Tic disorders

Tic disorders (e.g., motor tic, vocal tics, and Tourette's) are generally diagnosed during childhood and adolescence. They are categorized as neurodevelopmental disorders in DSM-5.

113. A social worker meets with a mother who has recently learned that her daughter was sexually abused by her stepfather, the woman's second husband, over a period of at least two years. The woman states she feels angry that her daughter disclosed the abuse to a guidance counselor instead of telling her. What information can the social worker tell the mother that might be helpful to her understanding why her daughter didn't tell?

There are many reasons children don't disclose abuse to family members. When the abuser is part of the family, children often worry they won't be believed, or that the family will break up as a result of the disclosure. Explaining the complexities of disclosure can help the mother understand why her daughter chose not to tell her about the stepfather's abuse.

A) Children usually feel more comfortable disclosing abuse to a professional rather than a parent.

   Children don't usually seek professional help to make disclosures of abuse.

B) Children sometimes don't disclose abuse to a parent, because of fears they won't be believed or the family might be destroyed.

   Children are often afraid of what might happen if they report abuse: getting in trouble, losing contact with the abuser, or breaking up the family.

C) Children almost always tell someone outside the family first before telling a parent.

   Children may or may not tell someone outside the family first. Parents are often the first to hear about the abuse.

D) Children usually tell someone at school, since they believe the information will be kept confidential.

   Children don't usually make disclosures of abuse at school.

114. A doctor has referred a woman to a social worker because the woman has been diagnosed with vaginismus. The treatment goals are MOST likely to address:

Vaginismus is a female sexual dysfunction in which involuntary muscle contraction causes pain during sexual activity. It has no physical cause and is usually related to anxiety about sexual intercourse. Vaginismus can be episodic or last a lifetime. Sometimes it's associated with a history of sexual abuse.

A) The woman's anxiety about having sex.

   Treating vaginismus usually involves addressing a woman's anxiety about sexual intercourse.

B) The woman's hypersexuality.

   Vaginismus refers to pain during sexual activity, not the degree of activity.

C) The woman's sexual promiscuity.

   Vaginismus refers to pain during sexual activity and is not related to sexual promiscuity.

D) The woman's lack of sexual desire.

   Vaginismus refers to pain during sexual activity and is not a function of a woman's libido.

115. A social worker meets with several clients at a local nursing home. A new resident to the facility has Parkinson's disease. What symptoms is the person likely to exhibit?

The symptoms of Parkinson's disease--tremors, slowed movement, rigid muscles, balance and posture problems, and speech changes--tend to start out mild and progress over time. No cure exists, but many of the symptoms can be managed with medication, and in some cases surgery.

A) Significant vision problems, loss of bowel control, depression, and memory problems.

   These symptoms are more indicative of multiple sclerosis.

B) Tremors, impaired balance, monotone speech, and hesitation prior to speaking.

   These are common symptoms that occur with Parkinson's disease.

C) Disorientation, wandering, delusions, and loss of inhibitions.

   These symptoms are more indicative of late-stage Alzheimer's disease.

D) Difficulty recognizing faces, decreased vision, and increased difficulty to adapt to low light levels.

   These symptoms are more indicative of macular degeneration.

116. Common symptoms during the beginning stages of Alzheimer's include:

Alzheimer's disease tends to start out with short-term memory problems, difficulty solving problems or recalling conversations, and a tendency to lose objects frequently. As the disease progresses, long-term memory is affected, and people lose the ability to read, write, and perform other tasks. Eventually, Alzheimer's it causes physical changes, such as mobility issues and incontinence.

A) Incontinence and difficulties with mobility.

Incontinence and lack of mobility are found in end-stage Alzheimer's.

B) Loss of previous skills such as reading and writing.

Loss of skills, such as the ability to read and write, are typical of the later stages of Alzheimer's.

C) Short-term memory loss and difficulty solving problems.

The earliest signs of Alzheimer's include short-term memory loss and difficulty solving problems.

D) Long-term memory loss and delusions.

Delusions--such as the belief that family members are stealing their money--and long-term memory loss are found in the later stages of Alzheimer's patients.

117. A social worker serves as a consultant to a local preschool program. The staff express concern about a four-year-old foster child who is very friendly with strangers. The child will often hug the parents of other children or start conversations with visitors to the preschool. What is MOST likely the reason for the child's behavior?

Children over nine months old who are overly friendly with strangers can be diagnosed with disinhibited social engagement disorder. The behavior used to be categorized as part of reactive attachment disorder, but gets its own diagnosis in DSM-5

A) The child most likely has an intellectual disability.

Behaving in an overly friendly manner toward strangers is not necessarily indicative of an intellectual disability.

B) The child may have disinhibited social engagement disorder.

Children with disinhibited social engagement disorder are overly friendly with strangers. Since this child is a foster child, it is possible that the disruption in caregivers may have led to attachment problems.

C) The child is likely an extrovert, so the behavior does not warrant concern.

Four-year-olds are normally shy around strangers. The child's overly friendly behavior is indicative of disinhibited social engagement disorder.

D) The child may have reactive attachment disorder.

> *In DSM-5, a child behaving in an overly friendly manner toward strangers can be diagnosed with disinhibited social engagement disorder.*

118. A hospital social worker is looking for a nursing home placement for an elderly woman. The woman has had a serious stroke and is no longer able to communicate or care for herself. What is the FIRST thing the social worker should do to help determine an appropriate placement for the woman?

When people complete a health care proxy, they often designate someone to make health care decisions in the event they become incapacitated. This is often also true of living wills. Before seeking guidance from family or doctors, the social worker should determine if the client's wishes have been recorded.

A) See if the patient has a spouse who is available to sign paperwork.

> *The social worker should first check to see if there is paperwork designating someone to make health care decisions--often, but not always, a spouse.*

B) Determine if the patient has a health care proxy or living will in place.

> *It's appropriate to discover whether or not the patient has already appointed someone to make health care decisions in the event she's incapacitated--a question usually covered in a health care proxy or living will.*

C) Meet with any available family members to obtain necessary signatures.

> *Since family dynamics may play a part in the decision, the social worker shouldn't leave the choice to whatever family members happen to be available.*

D) Speak with doctors about obtaining emergency guardianship for the patient.

> *Guardianship is probably not necessary at this point. It's more appropriate to determine if someone else has been designated to make health care decisions for the client.*

119. A 60-year-old man meets with a social worker in a community mental health center. The man states that he was widowed five years ago. He has started dating and was hoping to become intimate with his new partner. However, he has been experiencing erectile dysfunction for the first time, and wonders if it may be related to the guilt he feels about dating again. What should the social worker do FIRST?

Since erectile dysfunction can be caused by physical health issues, it's important to refer to a doctor to rule out these problems before treating erectile dysfunction as a mental health issue.

A) Recommend couples counseling with the man's partner to address their sexual issues.

There's no evidence that couples counseling is warranted.

B) Recommend a physical exam with his primary care doctor to rule out physical health issues.

Since this man may have underlying health issues, it's appropriate to refer him for a physical exam.

C) Explain that this is part of the normal aging process.

Although many men do experience erectile dysfunction as they age, before accepting he will always struggle with it, this man should first consult a doctor to rule out any underlying physical causes.

D) Establish treatment goals to resolve the man's underlying grief.

Although this man may be experiencing sexual problems due to his unresolved grief, physical health problems should be ruled out first.

120. A 14-year-old has been diagnosed with conduct disorder. The teenager also has a substance abuse problem. What disorder is the child MOST at risk for developing as an adult?

Childhood conduct disorder can lead to antisocial personality disorder in adulthood. This risk is increased if a child is using substances.

A) Major depression

Conduct disorder tends to progress into antisocial personality disorder in adulthood, not depression.

B) Histrionic personality disorder

Conduct disorder tends to progress into antisocial personality disorder in adulthood.

C) Antisocial personality disorder

Conduct disorder tends to progress into antisocial personality disorder in adulthood.

D) Narcissistic personality disorder

Conduct disorder tends to progress into antisocial personality disorder in adulthood.

121. A hospital social worker meets with family members of an 85-year-old woman with Alzheimer's disease. The woman's daughter would like to have her mother move in with her, because her mother is no longer able to care for herself. The daughter asks what things she can do to help care for her mother in her home. What is the MOST appropriate suggestion?

People caring for a family member with Alzheimer's disease need education about proper care, including how to adapt their home to prevent accidents and injuries.

A) The social worker should discuss ways in which the woman can teach her mother to perform tasks safely, such as using a microwave instead of the stove.

   People with Alzheimer's disease don't generally retain information, so teaching them new tasks isn't helpful.

B) The social worker should discuss ways of keeping the woman's mother from being bored or lonely, such as leaving the TV on a news channel during the day.

   People with Alzheimer's disease can become agitated by news stories, so this woman should not be encouraged to let her mother watch a news channel.

C) The social worker should discuss strategies--such as removing clutter--that the woman can use to make her home safer for her mother.

   Adapting the environment is the best way to help a person care for a family member with Alzheimer's disease.

D) Because caring for a person with dementia is a big responsibility, the social worker should discourage the woman from having her mother move in.

   After providing people with information about caring for an elderly family member, the social worker should leave the ultimate decision to the family.

122. Family therapy is usually LEAST appropriate in which of the following situations?

It's normal and healthy for teens to separate themselves from their parents during adolescence, so family therapy aimed at making the family more cohesive during this time usually isn't appropriate. If there are severe behavior problems, substance-abuse issues, or evidence of mental illness, family therapy may be warranted.

A) A 25-year-old woman requests her parents attend family therapy so they can better understand her depression.

   Long-term mental illness, such as serious depression, can often benefit from family therapy.

B) A 30-year-old woman is struggling with alcohol problems and she and her husband are requesting family therapy.

Family therapy can be very helpful for substance-abuse problems.

C) Parents request family therapy because their 16-year-old daughter seems to be pulling away from them.

It is developmentally appropriate for a teenager to begin pulling away from her parents and forge her own identity. Unless a teenager exhibits significant behavior problems or mental health issues, family therapy isn't warranted.

D) Parents request family therapy to help their newly adopted ten-year-old adjust to their home.

In cases of adoption, family therapy can help clarify expectations and facilitate relationships.

123. According to Erikson's psychosocial stages, if a child does not receive predictable and consistent care from a caregiver during his first year of life, he could be at risk for:

Erikson's psychosocial stages discuss human development throughout the lifespan. Erikson theorized that the first year of life was extremely important for developing a child's sense of trust or mistrust toward the world. If a caregiver is reliable, consistent and loving, a child will likely develop a sense of trust. If not, according to Erikson, a child can be at risk for mistrust the rest of his life.

A) Isolation.

Erikson's stage of "intimacy versus isolation" refers to young adults between 18 and 40--the stage in which people either develop successful long-term relationships with people outside the family or not.

B) Guilt.

Erikson's stage of "initiative versus guilt" refers to children between the ages of three and six, as they begin to ask adults questions by way of exploring their world.

C) Inferiority.

Erikson's stage of "industry versus inferiority" refers to children ages six to twelve, as they learn and master specific skills.

D) Mistrust.

Erikson's stage of "trust versus mistrust" begins at birth and lasts until age one--the stage in which babies either learn to trust caregivers or not.

124. A social worker meets with an adult male with mild intellectual disability. The man resides with his parents but states his goal is to live independently. He tells the social worker that he has met someone over the Internet and his plan is to move in with this person, even though they have never met. How should the social worker proceed?

Social workers should respect clients' right to self-determination in most cases. However, if a person's plan is potentially dangerous or if a person lacks the capacity to make healthy decisions, the social worker should use professional judgment when responding.

A) The social worker should help the client identify what services he will need when he moves.

> *Since the client might not end up moving, the social worker should not immediately begin linking the client to resources. Instead, the social worker should discuss potential risks involved and learn more about the plan.*

B) The social worker should point out potential risks associated with moving in with a stranger.

> *Pointing out the potential risks of moving in with a stranger is the best course here given safety concerns.*

C) The social worker should respect the man's right to self-determination and praise him for finding a way to live independently.

> *Safety concerns in this case eclipse the man's right to self-determination if the social worker thinks a could be dangerous. Since this man has intellectual disability, he is at risk of being taken advantage of. Moving in with a stranger is not likely in his best interest.*

D) The social worker should be outwardly supportive but should contact the man's family to discuss his plan.

> *Acting supportive to the client while expressing concern to the client's family would be deceptive and likely undermine the therapeutic relationship.*

125. A social worker is asked to serve on a board of directors at a local homeless shelter. The social worker would need to attend meetings outside normal business hours. The social worker is interested in the opportunity, which would be strictly voluntary. What is the BEST way for the social worker to respond to the request?

The NASW code of ethics is clear that service is an important social work value. Social workers should be willing to participate in some social work activities on a pro bono basis.

A) The social worker can participate, because social workers are encouraged to offer some services without pay.

> *The NASW Code of Ethics encourages social workers to volunteer some portion of their skills without payment, so it's appropriate for this social worker to volunteer.*

B) The social worker should agree to serve on the board, but only if the board will provide salary and malpractice coverage.

> *The NASW Code of Ethics encourages social workers to provide some services free of charge, so the social worker should not expect payment or insurance.*

C) The social worker should not engage in volunteer work as a professional, because it could expose the social worker to malpractice.

> *Social workers should take reasonable precautions to protect themselves against malpractice, but volunteer work does not necessarily open social workers up to lawsuits.*

D) The social worker should decline the request, because working more hours without pay will likely lead to burnout.

> *Although social workers should take steps to prevent burnout, offering some service for free is an aspect of social work clearly included in the NASW Code of Ethics.*

126. A social worker is employed in a medical facility. The social worker's role is to meet with people prior to their medical appointment and conduct any necessary screenings. When meeting with pregnant women, the social worker only asks about any current drug use when the patient is of a lower socioeconomic status. The social worker's actions:

A social worker's unwarranted assumptions based on people's class, religion, gender, or other factors can impact treatment and interfere with data gathering. Social workers should ask all pregnant women about their drug use, regardless of socioeconomic status. Pregnant women with higher education and incomes may still have drug or alcohol issues.

A) Are a good way to avoid offending middle- or upper-class women.

> *Social workers should ask questions in a matter-of- fact way so as to not offend, but shouldn't avoid asking questions that can yield crucial information, simply out of a reluctance to embarrass people of higher socioeconomic status.*

B) Show how a provider's values can interfere with appropriate screenings.

> *A social worker's biases, including the assumption that pregnant middle- or upper-class women don't use drugs, can have serious negative consequences.*

C) Are an efficient way to gather information, because women of higher socioeconomic status aren't likely to use drugs.

Women of all socioeconomic classes can have substance-abuse problems.

D) Are based on evidence-based practices.

Middle- or upper-class women may have drug or alcohol problems during pregnancy and social workers should never assume they don't.

127. A social worker volunteers at a local charity. One of the other volunteers invites her out on a date. The social worker knows this man is a brother of one of her current clients. What are the ethical implications for engaging in a romantic relationship with this man?

Social workers are not only obligated to avoid sexual contact with clients, but they should also not engage in relationships with clients' relatives when there's potential harm to the client.

A) The social worker should decline to go on the date, since it's likely to compromise the therapeutic relationship with the client.

It's ethically appropriate to decline an invitation to go on a date with a relative of a client.

B) The social worker should ask her client how he would feel if she went out on a date with his brother.

Entering into a sexual relationship with a client's brother is likely to impact the therapeutic relationship. It's up to the social worker to maintain appropriate boundaries, which would be violated by asking the client's tacit permission to go on the date.

C) The social worker is free to accept the invitation, but should talk to her client about how to ensure it doesn't impact their therapeutic relationship.

The social worker has a responsibility to avoid a sexual relationship with a client's relative, and the possible negative impact of such a relationship can't be gauged through advance discussion with the client.

D) Since the man is not her client, the social worker is free to engage in a romantic relationship with him.

Social workers should avoid entering into sexual relationships with the relatives of clients, especially when there's the risk of harm to the treatment .

128. While testifying in court, a social worker is asked her opinion about whether or not the defendant, her client, is capable of physically abusing her child. The social worker is MOST likely:

Social workers can serve as expert witnesses in court, can be hired by either the defense or the prosecution, and are entitled to receive payment for their testimony.

A) Acting outside of her scope of practice.

>   *There's no evidence the social worker is acting outside her scope of practice.*

B) A witness for the prosecution.

>   *The social worker may be testifying for the defense or the prosecution.*

C) Breaching confidentiality.

>   *Social workers will usually have obtained consent from a client to testify in court, or will have received a subpoena, so there's no reason to assume a breach of confidentiality.*

D) An expert witness.

>   *Since this social worker is being asked to render a professional opinion, she's most likely an expert witness.*

129. An eight-year-old child has started seeing a social worker. The social worker and the client's mother have agreed on once-a-week sessions, but the mother has canceled so many appointments the social worker has only seen the child about once a month for four months. The social worker reiterates that more sessions are needed to help the child, but despite her promises, the mother hasn't yet brought the child consistently. How should the social worker proceed?

If clients are not following through on established schedules, to the point where they're not benefiting from services, social workers can discharge clients from treatment.

A) To increase the child's attendance, the social worker should tell the mother the child needs to meet two times per week rather than one.

>   *Recommending the child attend two times per week isn't likely to increase the child's attendance, since the mother is already balking at the agreed-upon once-a-week schedule.*

B) The social worker should continue to see the child as often as the mother is able to take him to appointments.

>   *Since this social worker has made it clear that the child isn't benefiting from monthly sessions, the social worker should not continue to see the child.*

C) **Since the child isn't likely to benefit from being seen only once a month, the social worker should terminate the treatment.**

> *Since the social worker has made it clear that more frequent sessions are necessary, and the mother has failed to comply, the social worker should discharge the client.*

D) The social worker should tell the family to take a month off and think about whether or not they want treatment.

> *Telling the family to take a month off from treatment may be perceived as punishment, and inconsistent with the goal of seeing the child more often.*

130. A social worker is doing discharge planning at a medical hospital, referring patients to receive in-home care or nursing-home care following their discharge. A nursing home contacts the social worker, says they have several available beds, and offers the social worker a bonus for referring people to the nursing home. How should the social worker respond?

Since a social worker's primary responsibility is to the client, accepting compensation for referring clients to a particular service or agency is a conflict of interest, and therefore unethical.

A) **The social worker should decline any type of referral bonus from the nursing home.**

> *The social worker should decline the invitation and continue to make referrals that are in the best interest of the client.*

B) The social worker should accept the nursing home's invitation to receive referral bonuses and make referrals accordingly.

> *Social workers should not accept any type of compensation for making referrals.*

C) The social worker can accept the referral bonus, but should not allow it to influence decisions as to where people are referred upon discharge.

> *Receiving compensation for referring clients to a particular nursing home can compromise the social worker's ability to act in the best interest of clients.*

D) The social worker should inform a supervisor that the social worker is receiving compensation for the referral.

> *Accepting the referral bonus amounts to a conflict of interest.*

131. Which of the following is considered unethical behavior?

Social workers are not trained to give out medical advice. Recommending what medications are best for a client is out of social workers' scope of practice and is unethical.

A) Discharging clients who miss too many appointments.

Social workers are allowed to discharge clients who miss too many appointments if they have discussed the rules and consequences ahead of time.

B) Working only one day per week and not offering clients scheduling flexibility.

Social workers can choose to work whatever schedule they want, as long as they've made clients aware of the limitations of their schedule.

C) Charging clients for missed appointments.

Although many insurance companies don't allow people to be charged for missed appointments, social workers who accept self-pay clients may charge for missed appointments, provided clients are apprised of this ahead of time.

D) Advising a client which medications he should ask his doctor to prescribe.

Social workers should not be giving out medical advice, so telling a client which medication will work best is unethical.

132. A couple considering divorce meets with a social worker. They report arguing constantly and feeling hopeless about preserving the marriage. What is important for the social worker to share with the couple with regard to informed consent?

When people seek counseling for relationship issues, their problems may initially get worse. In accordance with the principle of informed consent, the social worker should advise the couple that treatment is voluntary and that discussing their problems may lead to increased discomfort and marital discord.

A) The social worker should recommend they both seek legal counsel, since session notes could be used in court if they decide to divorce.

Since divorce is being considered, but hasn't been decided upon, it's not necessary for the clients to obtain legal counsel at this point.

B) The social worker should recommend individual counseling in addition to couples counseling.

Although there may be circumstances in which it makes sense for people to seek individual counseling in addition to couples work, there's no indication this is necessary at this point.

C) The social worker should inform the couple that counseling runs the risk of increasing their marital discord, especially at first.

It's important to inform the couple that discussing their issues may cause additional argument and pain.

D) The social worker should inform the couple that because their relationship has deteriorated, counseling is not likely to be helpful.

Though it's true that counseling may further unravel the clients' marriage, the social worker shouldn't predict that counseling won't be helpful.

133. What should social workers be aware of in terms of malpractice cases?

Since social workers can be sued for malpractice--a potentially expensive ordeal--it's advisable to carry malpractice insurance, even if their employer also carries a malpractice policy.

A) Social workers cannot be sued for malpractice, but the company they work for can be.

Social work individuals can be sued, along with their agencies.

B) Social workers can be sued for malpractice and should carry malpractice insurance.

Since social workers can be sued for malpractice--for a variety of reasons--they should carry malpractice insurance.

C) Social workers can only be sued if they breach confidentiality.

A breach of confidentiality is only one of the many reasons social workers can be sued.

D) The social work licensing board will defend social workers who face legal issues, so social workers don't need separate malpractice insurance.

The licensing board doesn't offer protection to social workers sued for malpractice.

134. A social worker employed by a hospital faces an ethical dilemma regarding confidentiality. The hospital's policy conflicts with the NASW Code of Ethics. How should the social worker resolve the ethical dilemma?

When confronted with discrepancies between their agency's practices and the NASW Code of Ethics, social workers should strive to maintain behavior consistent with the code. If unable to resolve an issue successfully, a social worker should seek consultation.

A) The social worker should try to resolve the issue in a manner consistent with the Code of Ethics and seek consultation if necessary.

The Code of Ethics says that social workers should try to resolve ethical dilemmas in a manner consistent with the code.

B) The social worker should follow the hospital's policy in this instance but advocate for policy change in the future.

The social worker should not comply with the hospital policy if it means behaving in a manner inconsistent with the Code of Ethics.

C) The social worker should resign from the hospital.

If the social worker is able to maintain compliance with the NASW Code of Ethics, there's no need to resign. Resigning would be a last step.

D) The social worker should comply with the hospital's policy even if it contradicts the Code of Ethics.

The Code of Ethics is clear that social workers should strive to maintain behavior consistent with the code.

135. A hospice care social worker notices he's feeling overwhelmed by his work lately. He feels confused, exhausted, and has been having difficulty sleeping. The social worker suspects he may be experiencing burnout. What should he do FIRST?

Burnout, a common experience for social workers, can have a variety of causes, such as large caseloads and little support. Symptoms of burnout vary, but often include both emotional and physical symptoms that impact a person's job performance. If a social worker is experiencing burnout, it's important to talk immediately to a supervisor, colleagues, and other agency personnel to develop a plan of action, which can include reassignment, shifts in the schedule, or increased support.

A) The social worker should explain his burnout to his clients and apologize, since it's likely they haven't been getting good services lately.

The social worker should not burden clients with information about burnout.

B) The social worker should try to leave work an hour earlier so he doesn't feel so overwhelmed.

Although cutting back on hours may be helpful, it's more important to seek support from the agency, or perhaps even professional help, to address the problem.

C) The social worker should consult with a supervisor to discuss a plan of action to address his burnout.

It's important to address the issue in a timely fashion with people in the agency.

D) Since burnout often goes away within a few weeks, the social worker should wait to see if it passes in his case.

Burnout usually requires changes in lifestyle and does not go away on its own.

136. A dual relationship, in which a social worker interacts with a client on a social basis:

Though it's best practice to avoid dual relationships, which may require clients to be transferred, they're not always unethical and sometimes can't be avoided, especially in rural areas. Dual relationships are unethical when they're sexual in nature or exploit the client in some fashion.

A) Always requires a transfer to a new social worker.

Even if a dual relationship is present, there may be circumstances in which a social worker can maintain a professional relationship with a client.

B) Is always unethical.

Dual relationships are not always unethical, especially in rural settings.

C) Might not be unethical if it isn't sexual in nature.

There may be circumstances, especially in rural areas, where a dual relationship is unavoidable and does not harm the client.

D) Should always be avoided.

It's not always possible to avoid a dual relationship, especially in rural settings.

137. A social worker has met with a man for six sessions to address his grief. The man's wife passed away two years ago and he still cries whenever he tries to talk about her. After the sixth session, the man calls the social worker to say he's not making progress and would like to transfer to a female social worker. What should the social worker do?

Under most conditions, social workers should transfer clients when they wish to see a different social worker, and should assist with a referral.

A) Agree to discharge him from treatment and tell him he's welcome to find a new social worker.

In addition to discharging him, the social worker should offer to refer him to a different social worker rather than implying he's on his own.

B) Tell the man that he should continue for at least 12 sessions before deciding if he's making any progress.

> *If this client does not feel treatment is helpful, another six sessions isn't likely to change his mind.*

C) Explain that changing to a female social worker could be problematic since he's dealing with issues related to the loss of his wife.

> *If the man prefers a female social worker, a transfer is appropriate, and his grief issues don't rule out a female therapist.*

D) Give the man several choices of female social workers and offer to refer him to the one he selects.

> *It's appropriate to discharge the man and discuss referral options.*

138. A residential treatment program treats people with a combination of mental health and substance- abuse problems. The severity of the clients' issues has created a lot of problems, including assaults on staff members. The program director has decided to offer a token economy system, in which residents can earn tokens for positive behaviors, such as medication compliance and participation in group therapy, exchanging the tokens for toiletries, movies, or phone cards. In terms of ethics, what should the facility keep in mind?

Many hospitals and residential treatment centers that work with dually diagnosed patients use behavioral approaches to treatment, rewarding patients for participation and compliance. Staff should be appropriately trained to ensure that the system is applied in an ethical manner.

A) It's unethical to use a token economy system with adults, because the staff would be treating the residents like children.

> *Token economy systems can be used with adults in a respectful manner.*

B) It's unethical to link medication compliance to rewards, but appropriate to reward participation and compliance with other services.

> *It's acceptable to offer rewards for medication compliance.*

C) It's unethical to make rewards contingent on the client's participation or compliance with the program.

> *So long as the program is voluntary, it's ethical to offer rewards based on compliance.*

D) So long as staff are well-trained and the program is voluntary, a token economy system is ethical.

If staff are properly trained, and the system is applied in a consistent fashion, a reward program is ethical.

139. A social worker meets with a 45-year-old woman who discloses she was physically abused by her father when she was a child. She states that her father used to beat her with a belt and sometimes threatened to kill her. In terms of mandated reporting to child protective services, what is the social worker's responsibility?

Social workers need to make mandated reports when there is a suspicion of child abuse or neglect and the child may still be in danger. When adults reveal past incidents of abuse or neglect, there's no responsibility to make a report, unless another child is in danger.

A) The social worker needs to make a mandated report based on this woman's reports of childhood abuse.

Since the woman is an adult, the social worker doesn't need to make a mandated report.

B) The social worker doesn't need to make a mandated report, because there's no evidence any children are in imminent danger.

Unless there are still children who may be in danger, the social worker doesn't need to make a mandated report.

C) The social worker should consult with a supervisor to discuss the pros and cons of making the mandated report.

Since there's no evidence a child is in danger, there's no need to consult with a supervisor.

D) The social worker doesn't have a legal obligation to make a report, but making a report would be the ethical response.

The social worker has neither a legal nor an ethical obligation to make a mandated report.

140. A social worker has started to engage in a romantic relationship with another person who works at the office. Which of the following is true of co-worker relationships?

The Code of Ethics states that, "social workers should avoid engaging in sexual relationships with colleagues where there is potential for a conflict of interest." Social workers should also not allow romantic relationships to impact their performance, and should transfer responsibilities whenever necessary to avoid potential issues.

A) Social workers can engage in a romantic relationship with co-workers, as long as potential conflicts of interest are avoided.

> *Social workers are able to engage in romantic relationships with co-workers as long as they won't create a conflict of interest.*

B) Social workers can engage in romantic relationships with any colleague, except for a supervisor.

> *Social workers should avoid engaging in a romantic co-worker relationship that might create a conflict of interest. Supervisors are expressly forbidden from sexual relationships with supervisees in the NASW Code of Ethics.*

C) Social workers are not allowed to engage in any romantic relationships with co-workers.

> *Social workers are able to engage in romantic relationships with co-workers as long as there's no potential conflict of interest.*

D) Social workers cannot engage in relationships with clients but are free to engage in relationships with any colleagues they wish.

> *Social workers cannot engage in co-worker relationships that could present a conflict of interest.*

141. Which one of the following is MOST likely a breach of ethical conduct?

Self-disclosure should be used sparingly with clients, and only in their best interests. When disclosing personal information, a social worker should receive consultation and supervision to discuss possible ethical issues and rule out telling a client anything potentially harmful.

A) Despite having a release of information for a psychiatrist, the social worker reviews the information with the client prior to releasing it.

> *There may be good reasons for a social worker to review the information with the client, even when there's a release on file.*

B) The social worker has to cancel two appointments in a row due to illness.

> *So long as the social worker makes arrangements to reschedule appointments, there's nothing unethical about canceling appointments due to illness or for other pressing reasons.*

C) A social worker discloses personal tragedy to a client.

Disclosing personal tragedy to a client could be harmful and should only be done with extreme caution.

D) A social worker discusses movies with a client.

Talking about movies could be part of developing a therapeutic relationship or may have a therapeutic purpose, such as discussing the way mental illness is portrayed in media and the impact if those portrayals.

142. A certain substance-abuse treatment program provides services to homeless people. Because their homelessness often interferes with their ability to attend outpatient services regularly, the social work director decides to offer housing to the people who attend the program, stipulating that anyone who tests positive for drugs will be immediately evicted. What are the ethical ramifications of making abstinence a stipulation for housing?

Not only is it ethical for substance-abuse programs to require abstinence in return for services, including housing, research shows that this requirement can be an effective intervention, provided participants know the rules, risks, and benefits in advance.

A) Making abstinence a condition for housing is ethical, but funding for such a program is likely to be impossible.

Since research has shown that such a condition can be an effective form of treatment, many insurance carriers, grants and private funding sources are likely to support such a program.

B) It's unethical to evict anyone for testing positive for drugs.

As long as participants are made aware of the stipulations, it's ethical to make abstinence a condition for housing.

C) It's unethical to randomly drug test the people living in the housing units.

So long as participants are aware that abstinence is a condition of treatment, it's ethical to perform random drug tests.

D) It's ethical to make abstinence a stipulation for housing.

If clients know the rules in advance, it's ethical to make drug-testing and abstinence conditions of housing.

143. A social worker is filling out a form for a client, in ink, that documents the client's diagnosis and treatment goals. The social worker incorrectly writes the diagnosis as generalized anxiety

disorder, then remembers the diagnosis is actually social anxiety disorder. What is the BEST way for the social worker to deal with the error?

When documenting an error on a legal document, social workers should put a line through the error, date and initial it, and write the word "error," before adding the correct information.

A) The social worker should put a line through the error, initial and date it, write the word "error," and then add the change.

> *It's appropriate to note the error, draw a line through it, leaving it legible. The error should be initialed and dated.*

B) The social worker should write a letter explaining the error and staple it to the original form.

> *The mistake can be corrected on the form, so the social worker doesn't have to append a letter.*

C) Since the error can't be fixed, the social worker should ask the client for a new copy of the form.

> *The social worker doesn't need to complete an entirely new form.*

D) The social worker should use white-out to cover up the mistake and then write the correct diagnosis.

> *Social workers should not use white-out on legal documents. Anyone reviewing the document should be able to see the error clearly.*

144. A social worker works in a busy private practice. When a client fails to show for an appointment, in terms of billing, the social worker MOST likely:

In most cases, billing the insurance company for services not rendered constitutes fraud. To reduce the incidence of missed appointments, social workers can create policies that encourage clients to show up for sessions.

A) Can only bill the insurance company if it's Medicaid.

> *Medicaid doesn't pay for appointments clients don't attend.*

B) Can only bill the insurance company for a partial amount.

> *Unless an insurance company offers the option, social workers cannot bill for a partial amount of the session if the client doesn't show up.*

C) Cannot bill the insurance company.

With most insurance companies, social workers cannot bill unless the client shows up for the appointment.

D) Can bill the insurance company for the full cost of the session.

With rare exceptions, no-show appointments cannot be billed to the insurance company.

145. A father takes his seven-year-old son to see a social worker in a community mental health center. The father states that his son is struggling to deal with the ongoing custody dispute. Currently the father has primary residence and the child visits with his mother every other weekend, but the mother wants primary residence and is taking the case back to court. The father thinks the child's mother may want the social worker to testify in court. What information should the social worker discuss with the child's father at the time of the assessment?

If a social worker is asked to provide treatment for a child, but is likely to be subpoenaed to discuss recommendations about the child's living situation, this potential conflict of interest should be discussed in advance with the family. A social worker providing treatment should not offer to be an expert witness.

A) The social worker should volunteer to testify on the father's behalf.

The social worker doesn't have enough information to say what is in the child's best interest at the time of the assessment, and if subsequently providing treatment, should not offer to testify on the father's behalf.

B) The father should be made aware of the social worker's role in treatment and the potential conflict of interest if the social worker is subpoenaed.

The code of ethics is clear that social workers should make clients aware of potential conflicts of interest, including when a therapist may be asked to testify about a child's living situation.

C) The social worker should gather information about the child's best interest so a recommendation can be made to the court.

If the social worker is hired to treat the client, the social worker should not focus on gathering evidence during treatment sessions.

D) The social worker should offer to treat the child while evaluating what's in the child's best interest.

Because of the potential conflict of interest, the social worker shouldn't volunteer to take on both roles.

146. A client meets with a social worker to discuss a variety of issues. The client talks about past trauma, a substance abuse problem, relationship issues, and financial problems. The client goes back and forth between problems and seems overwhelmed, however, she continuously talks about how her relationship problem with her spouse is most troubling to her. Which intervention is likely to be MOST helpful in identifying treatment goals?

Partializing is a way to help clients break down a lot of information into smaller units. By breaking down lots of problems into smaller steps, social workers can assist clients with developing strategies to address them one at a time.

A) Creating a genogram

   Creating a genogram is a tool that could help gather information but isn't likely to help her find solutions.

B) Supportive counseling

   Supportive counseling may cause this woman to feel better initially but is not likely to help her in the long-term and isn't likely to help her find solutions.

C) Reflective listening

   Reflecting back all of her problems may make her feel overwhelmed and isn't likely to help her begin finding solutions.

D) Partializing

   Partializing would help the client determine which problem to begin addressing.

147. A social worker at an outpatient mental health center conducts an intake on an eight-year-old child. The family's life is too chaotic for the child to benefit from outpatient services. The social worker's current agency does not provide in-home services, so a referral to a different agency is indicated. What is the BEST way for the social worker to proceed?

The NASW Code of Ethics is clear that social workers should not abandon clients when terminating services. When transferring a client to another service or agency, it's important to follow up to ensure that the referral was successful. Otherwise, clients can feel abandoned or fall between the cracks, due to problems with insurance, long waiting lists, or other complications.

A) If the family agrees to the referral, the social worker should make the referral, discharge the client, and follow up with the family to ensure the referral was successful.

   It is appropriate for the social worker to make the referral and then follow up to ensure that the client is able to start the new services.

B) Since the agency doesn't provide in-home services, the social worker should continue to provide outpatient services and try to meet the family's needs.

Since the social worker has already determined that outpatient services are inappropriate, the correct course is to refer to an agency that can meet the client's needs.

C) If the family agrees, the social worker should make the referral to the other agency and discharge the child from outpatient services.

The social worker should not only make the referral, but also follow up to make sure the new agency is able to provide the needed services.

D) The social worker should provide the family with the phone number for the agency that can provide in-home services, and encourage them to call.

Giving the family the phone number and discharging them may make them feel abandoned. Instead, the social worker should make the referral if the family agrees and the social worker should follow through to ensure that services are able to begin with the family.

148. A social worker in a rural practice setting has met with a client three times. During the fourth meeting, the client begins talking about her stepdaughter, whom the social worker now realizes he is also treating. Neither the woman nor her stepdaughter seems aware that they're both seeing the same therapist. How should the social worker proceed?

Social workers may end up treating various extended family members, especially in a rural setting. When situations arise that pose a conflict of interest, social workers need to refer clients to another therapist, while being careful not to breach confidentiality.

A) The social worker should transfer the woman to a new social worker and furnish her with names of available providers.

The social worker should make it clear the woman needs to see another therapist, and offer a list of treatment providers, but should refrain from breaching confidentiality by giving the specific reason for the transfer.

B) The social worker should explain the situation to the stepdaughter's biological mother and recommend the stepdaughter seek services elsewhere.

Speaking to the biological mother about her daughter's treatment would be a breach of confidentiality.

C) Since treatment has already begun, the social worker should continue to meet with the woman.

> *Because of the potential conflict of interest, the social worker should advise the client to see another therapist.*

D) The social worker should hold a meeting with the woman and her stepdaughter to discuss treatment options.

> *Since it appears this woman is not aware that her stepdaughter is being treated by the social worker, holding a joint meeting would constitute a breach of confidentiality.*

149. A client is being treated for social phobia. When completing the treatment plan, the social worker wants to include objective data. Which one of the following treatment goals is based on objective data?

In devising treatment plans, social workers need to be clear on how progress will be measured. There may be times when objective evidence is needed in addition to subjective statements from the client.

A) The client will attend church once a week.

> *Church attendance is something that can be clearly measured.*

B) The client will keep a journal that documents anxiety ratings on a daily basis.

> *Since a client's reports on feelings cannot be verified by others, this documentation is subjective rather than objective.*

C) The client will self-report reduced feelings of anxiety during therapy appointments.

> *The client's self-reports are based on subjective data about the client's feelings and cannot be measured by others.*

D) The client will report a better understanding of anxiety.

> *Offering a test to measure the client's understanding of anxiety, initially and later on, would yield objective results, but a client's report is purely subjective.*

150. A woman was referred to a social worker by her primary care physician because she has diabetes and doesn't take care to manage her blood sugar. The woman states she's depressed, forgets to test her blood sugar, and doesn't really like taking her medication. Who should establish the treatment goals for the treatment plan?

In general, social workers and clients should establish treatment goals together. The client needs to agree to the treatment goals and the social worker needs to be willing to help the client reach those goals. Although it may make sense to collaborate with the referral source, ultimately the person making the referral should not control the treatment goals.

A) The physician who made the referral

> *The physician who made the referral can be consulted and the physician's concerns discussed, but the client's goals should not be determined by the physician.*

B) The client

> *The client needs to be invested in the goals, but the social worker's professional expertise should also be included in the process.*

C) The social worker

> *The social worker should help establish the treatment goals, but the treatment will not be effective unless the client is invested in reaching those goals.*

D) The social worker and client

> *It's appropriate for the social worker and the client to work together to establish the objectives of treatment.*

151. Providing clients with information on how to get help when you're away from the office, and giving them access to 24-hour daily coverage:

Offering clients information about how to seek help 24 hours per day is best practice and can reduce a client's risk for suicide. This may entail providing phone numbers for a crisis hotline that clients can call when they aren't able to see the social worker.

A) Is not usually practical because most social workers aren't able to offer such information.

> *Suicide hotline and crisis numbers are generally available, and it's best practice for social workers to provide them.*

B) Can reduce a client's risk for suicide and is part of best practice.

> *Giving people access to emergency phone numbers is appropriate, since it can reduce a client's suicide risk.*

C) Can be unethical, because clients may become dependent on the 24-hour coverage rather than working through problems on their own.

Allowing people access to crisis numbers isn't likely to foster dependence, and can provide valuable help in an emergency.

D) Requires social workers to offer clients their personal phone numbers so they can be contacted in the event of an emergency.

Giving out personal phone numbers may cross ethical boundaries, but clients should be aware of how to seek help in the event of an emergency, such as calling a statewide crisis number.

152. A social worker meets with a client who is seeking treatment for generalized anxiety. The client is interested in including some non-traditional approaches to addressing the anxiety. What is the treatment plan MOST LIKELY to include?

Sometimes people prefer to try less traditional methods to address their mental health issues. In particular, people who aren't interested in medication may benefit from alternative methods to address their anxiety, including relaxation, exercise, yoga, meditation, and breathing techniques.

A) Medication

Medication is considered a traditional choice to treat mental health disorders.

B) Eye movement desensitization and reprocessing

Although less common than many other types of therapy, EMDR is not considered an alternative approach. It's not commonly used to treat generalized anxiety, but rather to help people work through traumatic memories.

C) Yoga and breathing techniques

Yoga and breathing techniques are both considered alternative approaches to treating anxiety.

D) Psychoanalytic therapy

Psychoanalytic therapy is a commonly practiced treatment strategy. It is not considered a non-traditional treatment.

153. A social worker is working with a client who has been diagnosed with PTSD after getting into a serious car accident. In the course of establishing treatment plan goals, the social worker stresses the importance of discussing the car accident in detail during therapy sessions. What is the social worker's MOST likely intent?

One of the most common treatments for PTSD is exposure therapy. Talking in great detail about traumatic events can desensitize people to the trauma. It's often necessary for clients to discuss the traumatic event repeatedly until their distress decreases.

A) The social worker wants to help the client develop a story about the accident by using narrative therapy.

> *Although narrative therapy is sometimes used to treat PTSD, the emphasis in narrative therapy is on sharing a story rather than on repeatedly going over details.*

B) The social worker wants to use exposure therapy to reduce the client's distress about the accident.

> *In exposure therapy for PTSD, a social worker encourages the client to discuss details of the traumatic event, with the goal of desensitizing the client to the trauma.*

C) The social worker is likely hoping to witness what coping skills the client uses when discussing distressing events.

> *The point of repeatedly discussing the details of a traumatic event is to desensitize the client to the trauma, not simply to display the client's coping skills.*

D) The social worker wants to gather as much information as possible about the accident to gain a clear picture of the event.

> *The aim of the therapy is to lessen the client's distress through repeated discussion, not to grill the client into providing a full account of the event.*

154. A depressed client states he's not interested in taking medication to reduce his depression. The social worker recommends the client begin exercising as part of his treatment plan. The social worker's treatment recommendation is:

As long as a client is healthy enough to participate in exercise, social workers should recommend increasing physical activity as part of a client's treatment plan. In cases of depression, many studies have shown that exercise is an effective alternative or addition to medication.

A) Inappropriate, since only the client's doctor should be recommending changes to the client's physical activity.

> *There's no indication that the client is in poor health and would need a doctor's permission to increase his activity level.*

B) Likely to improve the client's overall physical health but unlikely to have any impact on the client's mental health.

> *Exercise can have positive benefits for both physical and mental health.*

C) Appropriate, since it's likely to help reduce the client's depression.

> *Exercise has been shown to reduce mild to moderate depression in many studies.*

D) Risky, as the client may experience side effects that can actually increase the depression.

> *Although people who begin exercising may experience side effects such as muscle soreness, it's unlikely that exercise will negatively impact the client's mood.*

155. A social worker in a community mental health center has a caseload of about 30 active clients. The social worker plans to go on maternity leave for at least six weeks. How should the social worker handle this absence?

Social workers should handle interruptions in service by giving clients as much advance notice as possible, providing information on how to seek help during the social worker's absence or, if the client so chooses, discontinuing therapy or transferring to a new social worker for ongoing treatment.

A) Each client should be given options about waiting, discharge, or referral to a different social worker.

> *The appropriate course is to discuss fully a client's options, including the pros and cons of each choice.*

B) Clients should be told the date when the social worker will be returning so they can resume treatment after her absence.

> *The social worker should not assume that all clients will want to wait for her to return, but should be given the option to transfer to a different social worker.*

C) The social worker should provide clients with a phone number where she can be reached during her absence from the office.

> *Clients should not be given the social worker's personal phone number. Instead, the social worker should provide information on resources that can be helpful during her absence.*

D) Clients should be discharged and referred to social workers who will be able to continue their treatment.

Since some clients may prefer to be discharged and not continue any treatment, while others may want to wait for the social worker to return, the social worker should not transfer everyone on her caseload.

156. A social worker meets with a man with a 25-year history of very heavy drinking. The man continues to drink daily but states he wants to quit. What level of care is likely MOST appropriate as a first step?

People with a long history of alcohol dependence may face serious medical complications as they begin to withdraw from alcohol. They may have many other physical health problems, such as high blood pressure. Withdrawing from alcohol can lead to seizures and even death, so initial detox should take place under the guidance of a physician.

A) Self-help groups

Since this man may experience life-threatening complications as he detoxes, medical treatment is the first priority.

B) Partial hospitalization program

A partial hospitalization program is likely able to help with the man's emotional needs, but may not effectively manage his physical health as he detoxes.

C) Acute medical hospitalization

Since this man may experience life-threatening withdrawal symptoms, acute medical care is the most appropriate option.

D) Residential treatment program

Medical treatment is the first priority, because this man could have serious physical complications as he detoxes from alcohol.

157. A social worker is employed as a case manager for a community mental health center. The agency is very busy and has recently been receiving increased referrals for case management. As a result, the social worker's caseload has doubled. What is the BEST way for the social worker to respond?

The NASW is clear that social workers should not have caseloads so large that they're unable to provide service of high quality to clients. If a social worker feels that caseload sizes are a burden, the social worker should advocate for change.

A) **The social worker should advocate for a smaller caseload to ensure that everyone is getting the services they need.**

> *Before taking on new clients, the social worker should advocate for smaller caseloads, to ensure that existing clients are getting their needs met.*

B) The social worker should prioritize the new referrals by scheduling their initial appointments, even if it means that established clients will have to miss appointments.

> *The social worker needs to provide high-quality services to existing clients before accepting new referrals.*

C) The social worker should space out the clients' sessions to ensure that everyone can be seen, even if appointments can only take place every other week.

> *If the social worker is unable to meet with clients as often as necessary, the social worker should not continue to accept new referrals.*

D) The social worker should seek professional consultation about which clients should be prioritized, to ensure that the social worker's feelings about clients aren't interfering with scheduling.

> *Although it may be helpful to seek consultation to prioritize existing clients, it's more appropriate to advocate that no new referrals be accepted until everyone is getting the services they need.*

158. A social worker employed as a case manager works at a homeless shelter, helping families find affordable housing, and linking families to various mental health, substance-abuse, employment and social service programs. In terms of record keeping, what is the case manager's responsibility?

The NASW is clear that case managers need to keep accurate records of all case-management activities. Whether a social worker provides clinical services or case management, notes must be kept either electronically or on paper to document the services provided.

A) The social worker only needs to keep records if the client's insurance is being billed.

> *Social workers need to keep records on clients regardless of whether or not the client has insurance.*

B) **The social worker needs to keep client records and all case management activities need to be documented.**

> *The NASW is clear that case managers need to keep accurate and timely documentation.*

C) The social worker should keep statistical records to help the homeless shelter obtain funding.

Although statistical information may help obtain funding, the primary reason to keep accurate records is to benefit clients.

D) Social workers who are employed as case managers do not need to keep any records.

Case managers must keep accurate records.

159. The director of social work at an acute care hospital wants to evaluate the effectiveness of the department's social workers. What would likely be the BEST way for the director to measure each social worker's performance?

The metrics used to evaluate a social worker's performance include how many days patients remain in the acute care setting, how long it takes for social work services to be initiated, and the number of readmissions with social complications.

A) The director could randomly survey former patients and ask if they were satisfied with the social work services they received during their hospital stay.

Randomly surveying patients might not provide an accurate look at how well the social worker is doing. Patients discharged to nursing homes, for example, may not be able to complete paperwork, or offer any real insight into the social worker's performance.

B) The director could use criteria such as how many days patients remain inpatient after being medically discharged, as well as the amount of time it takes for patients to receive social work services.

A statistical analysis can give the director a non-biased insight into each social worker's performance.

C) The director could ask each social worker to complete a self-evaluation form.

Although self-evaluation can offer insights into a social worker's strengths and weaknesses, it doesn't tell the director how the social worker's performance compares to the other social workers'.

D) The director could ask social workers to evaluate each other's performance.

Since friendships and personal issues among co-workers can get in the way, asking social workers to evaluate one another isn't likely to yield objective results.

160. A group of hospital social workers decide to give clients evaluation forms and comment cards after they've been discharged to learn more about their experience with treatment. Clients are told they don't have to fill out the forms or sign them. The social workers' actions are:

Social workers should take measures to evaluate their performance, which may include taking direct surveys from clients.

A) A good way to collect data to help evaluate their effectiveness.

> *Collecting data from clients can help consolidate their experiences in treatment and provide the social worker with useful information.*

B) Unethical, because clients shouldn't be asked to give feedback.

> *Asking clients about their experiences in treatment is an ethical practice.*

C) Not likely to be helpful, since clients aren't likely to give honest feedback.

> *Since the surveys are optional and likely anonymous, the feedback should be valuable.*

D) Not likely to be helpful, because clients often feel worse after treatment and may rate the social workers' performance negatively.

> *Although sometimes clients may experience increased symptoms initially, treatment should eventually help them feel better, and the survey design should reflect both possibilities.*

161. A social worker in private practice decides to establish a rule barring contact with clients outside of their appointments. All scheduling and rescheduling issues will be handled by the receptionist, and all other issues will need to wait until the next appointment. Establishing such a rule:

Establishing a rigid rule that clients can only have contact with the social worker during appointments can be damaging to the therapeutic relationship, and ignores the fact that clients may have crises or questions that require contact outside of normal treatment times.

A) Is a healthy boundary to set with all clients.

> *Establishing a rigid rule can be damaging to the therapeutic relationship, since clients may have valid reasons for contacting the social worker between appointments.*

B) Is a good way to prevent social work burnout.

> *Not allowing contact in between sessions may frustrate clients, cause them to be upset with the social worker during appointments, and actually increase burnout.*

C) **Can damage the therapeutic relationship.**

> *Not allowing any contact between appointments can be damaging to therapeutic rapport, whereas allowing a certain amount of contact can contribute to the therapeutic relationship.*

D) Is a good way to ensure clients don't become overly dependent.

> *Social workers should find a balance between allowing clients too much contact outside of treatment and not having any contact at all. An appropriate amount of contact can actually foster independence.*

162. One of the best ways to make the termination process MOST successful is:

The termination process should be handled carefully by social workers to prevent clients from feeling abandoned. Reviewing the gains a client has made, and linking them with natural supports they can access after treatment, are good ways to ensure successful termination.

A) **To link clients to social supports and review the gains made in treatment.**

> *Linking clients to natural supports and reviewing their progress can help make termination successful.*

B) To allow the client to make decisions about when to end treatment.

> *Some clients try to remain in treatment as long as possible, to avoid experiencing the loss associated with termination. Others try to deal with dependency issues by asking to terminate prematurely.*

C) To gradually decrease contact over the course of several months so that the client won't feel abandoned.

> *Gradually decreasing sessions can sometimes be helpful, but risks fostering dependency on the social worker if it drags out too long.*

D) To keep treatment brief so that the client won't become dependent or overly attached.

> *Sometimes long-term treatment is necessary, so only giving clients brief treatment is inappropriate.*

163. A social worker is working with a woman who was physically and emotionally abused during her childhood by both her mother and father. The woman makes frequent comments to the social worker along the lines of, "I'm sure you'll lie to me like everyone else in my life." In the interest of building trust, what is the BEST way for the social worker to respond to this type of statement?

People with a trauma history commonly have trust issues, and often experience transference in therapy, making it harder for a social worker to establish trust. To build trust over time, social workers should remain consistent with these clients and provide unconditional positive regard.

A) The social worker should set limits with the client, making it clear that such statements are not allowed.

> *So long as the client's comments aren't threatening or abusive, the social worker should allow the client to express concerns and fears about the treatment.*

B) The social worker should confront the client directly about these comments.

> *Confrontation is apt to meet with defensive resistance, and is unlikely to help foster the therapeutic relationship.*

C) The social worker should offer to transfer the client to a different social worker.

> *Transferring the client to a new social worker may cause the client to feel abandoned, leading to further trust issues.*

D) The social worker should remain consistent and nonjudgmental to help the client gradually work through trust issues.

> *To help the client build trust over time, the social worker should behave consistently and offer unconditional positive regard.*

164. A social worker meets with a couple who have been experiencing relationship issues connected with the wife's heavy drinking. The husband states he frequently tells his wife to stop and sometimes tries to hide her alcohol. How should the social worker proceed?

If a social worker has experience both in treating substance abuse and working with couples, it often makes sense to treat these issues simultaneously.

A) Recommend that the husband seek individual treatment to learn how to stop enabling his wife.

> *As a part of the couples therapy, the social worker can help the husband find ways to reduce any behavior that encourages his wife's drinking.*

B) Tell them they can't begin couples therapy until the wife gains control over her substance abuse.

> *The substance-abuse issues and marital issues don't have to be treated independently. Addressing the marital issues might reduce the substance abuse and vice versa.*

C) **Begin seeing them as a couple to address the substance-abuse problems and relationship issues.**

> *Behavioral couples therapy has been shown to be effective in reducing substance-abuse issues and related relationship problems.*

D) Tell the couple they can return for treatment after they both attend 12-step meetings for one month.

> *If the social worker gives the couple conditions to meet before they can begin treatment, they may be discouraged from seeking help.*

165. An eight-year-old child has been meeting with a social worker each week for six months to address his trauma. The child was inside a building when a tornado hit and later developed symptoms of PTSD. The child's symptoms have resolved and he's met his treatment goals. What is the BEST way for the social worker to proceed?

The termination process with children should foster their independence and help them maintain the progress they have made. Social workers can facilitate a positive transition by scheduling a graduation or celebration at the end of therapy.

A) **The social worker should schedule a "graduation" appointment and celebrate the child's progress prior to discharge.**

> *Celebrating the child's progress by scheduling a graduation session can help make the termination a positive experience.*

B) The social worker should continue to see the child weekly, because termination at this stage is likely to cause the child to regress.

> *If the child has met his treatment goals, and is unlikely to regress, the social worker should instill independence by ending treatment.*

C) The social worker should leave rescheduling open-ended, by telling the parent to call when a problem arises.

> *Leaving treatment open-ended isn't the proper way for the social worker and the child to say goodbye.*

D) The social worker should space the child's sessions out to once a month so the child will continue to have support available.

> *Continuing treatment after a child has met his treatment goals may send the message that the child needs the social worker, thereby fostering dependence.*

166. When it comes to establishing boundaries in a therapeutic relationship, the social worker should:

Boundaries in a therapeutic relationship are not fixed or absolute, and differ according to various factors, including age and setting. Boundaries with small children are not the same as boundaries with adults; boundaries in an acute medical facility will be different from those in a sex offender group, and so on.

A) Take each client's social and cultural factors into account when determining how to maintain healthy boundaries.

> *A person's culture, sex, religion, age, and mental health should all play a role in determining appropriate boundaries.*

B) Offer the client a list of acceptable and unacceptable behaviors so the client is clear about boundaries.

> *Although it can be helpful to discuss boundary issues, such as the difference between a therapeutic relationship and a friendship, there's no fixed list of rules that apply to all clients in all situations.*

C) Create a fixed list of rules about boundaries to ensure that violations do not occur.

> *It's impossible to create a fixed list of boundaries, because appropriate boundaries depend on the client, the therapeutic setting, and the situation.*

D) Ask for the agency's policies on boundaries and follow those rules when developing a therapeutic relationship.

> *Although agencies should offer guidelines for appropriate boundaries, there are few fixed rules that apply to all situations.*

167. A social worker talks to a supervisor about a child who's been placed in foster care. Before the child was removed from home, the social worker made several reports to child protective services about neglect. The social worker states he recently had a dream about the client. What is the therapist MOST likely experiencing?

Countertransference can appear in many forms, including thinking or talking a lot about a client outside of treatment, or dreaming about a client. Countertransference is especially common with social workers who deal with children. The neglect or abuse the child has suffered may trigger strong emotions, and lead the social worker to want to "save" the child.

A) A dual relationship with the client.

> *There's no indication of a dual relationship here.*

B) A subconscious way of working out therapeutic issues with the child.

Spending a great deal of time thinking about clients or dreaming about them is unlikely to contribute, consciously or unconsciously, to successful treatment.

C) A normal reaction to the child's change in caregiver.

Dreaming about clients is usually a sign of countertransference.

D) Countertransference about the child.

Dreaming about a client is often a sign the social worker has strong feelings about a client, and may be experiencing countertransference.

168. A social worker is working with a woman who discloses her long history of sexual abuse by an uncle. The woman says she's never told anyone about the abuse, largely due to her guilt and shame at having sometimes sought out her uncle and taken pleasure in the abuse. What is the BEST way for the social worker to respond to show empathy?

When showing empathy, it's important to identify the client's emotions and, rather than try to change those feelings, restate them to the client without judgment.

A) "Child abuse is never the child's fault."

Although this is a true statement, it doesn't reflect back what the client has said, and therefore doesn't show empathy.

B) "I know how you feel."

Telling a client you know how they feel is a statement about yourself, not a reflection of what the client is feeling.

C) "You feel ashamed because there were times you liked the abuse."

Reflecting how the client feels, without judging the client, shows empathy.

D) "You shouldn't feel ashamed. You were just a child."

Telling the client how she should or shouldn't feel doesn't show empathy.

169. A social worker has been making progress with a woman who wants help managing her anxiety and depression. After several sessions, the woman reports that she got into a physical altercation with her boyfriend a few days ago. Her 7-year-old and 9-year-old children were present, and one was cut by flying debris of a plate broken during the fight. The social worker

wants to make a report to child protective services. What can the social worker do to reduce the risk that making the report will damage the therapeutic relationship?

Making mandated reports about child abuse does run the risk for damaging the therapeutic relationship. A client who confides in a social worker about an incident or event may be upset to learn that a report is being made. One way to decrease any damage to the relationship is to offer clients to make a self-report directly from the social worker's office. If clients agree to this, it can empower them to be aware of what has been reported and provide them with more information about what to expect which can inspire more trust in the social worker.

A) The social worker should inform the client that her children are in danger of being removed from her but remind the client that the social worker is there to help.

> *Reminding the client that she may be in danger of losing her children is likely to seem like a threat and is not likely to help the therapeutic relationship.*

B) The social worker can give the woman a warning and tell her that if another incident happens, a report will need to be made.

> *If a social worker suspects abuse or neglect, a mandated report needs to be made. The social worker cannot offer a warning.*

C) **The social worker can encourage the mother to make a self-report from the social worker's office.**

> *Encouraging a self-report can help the client feel more empowered. It can also help the client maintain more trust when she is aware that the social worker is not secretly making the report.*

D) The social worker should make the report anonymously so that no one will know the social worker made the report.

> *Disruptive, Impulse-Control, and Conduct Disorders*

170. A social worker in an outpatient mental health center is using cognitive behavioral therapy to help a man with a history of depression and alcohol abuse. The man arrives for an appointment and appears to be under the influence of alcohol. When the social worker asks the man if he's been drinking, he replies, "I had three beers today but it was several hours ago." The social worker cancels the man's appointment and asks him to attend the next appointment sober. Canceling this man's appointment:

Establishing a healthy therapeutic relationship includes setting limits to unhealthy behavior in the treatment setting. When clients attend appointments under the influence of substances, it's appropriate for social workers to cancel the appointment and reschedule. Clients are unlikely to retain information or benefit from outpatient treatment if they're impaired.

A) Is an appropriate way to set limits and establish a healthy therapeutic relationship.

Developing a healthy therapeutic relationship depends in part on setting limits to a client's unhealthy behavior in a treatment setting.

B) Is likely to feel punitive to this man and could be very damaging to his treatment goals.

The social worker should let the man know that showing up intoxicated is unacceptable behavior.

C) Is unwarranted, because the man states he only had three beers, several hours ago, and can still benefit from the session. .

Since this man still appears to be under the influence of alcohol, it's unlikely he'll be able to participate actively in cognitive behavioral therapy.

D) Is unethical, because the man is entitled to the appointment.

Setting limits to a client's behavior isn't unethical.

Thanks for studying with SWTP! For more practice questions and to receive our free study guide, visit socialworktestprep.com.

If you have any questions, please don't hesitate to contact us:
info@socialworktestprep.com

Good luck on the exam!

Made in the USA
Monee, IL
07 June 2020